# Cow Country Cuisine
## 2ND EDITION

ക്കൗ

# Cow Country Cuisine
## 2nd Edition

*By Kathy McCraine*
*Illustrations and Photographs by the Author*

ക്കൗ

Published by K8 Communications

ℰℛ

# INTRODUCTION

It's been more than 25 years since *Cow Country Cuisine*, now out of print, was first published as a hardback cookbook. In 1988 I teamed up with the Arizona State Cowbelles (the women's auxiliary to the Arizona Cattle Growers' Association) and the International Brangus Auxiliary (auxiliary to the International Brangus Breeders Association) to collect recipes and distribute a book that would promote the nutritional value and sheer deliciousness of including beef in a healthy diet.

A lot has changed in the publishing world since then, most notably the skyrocketing popularity of e-books. So, when my colleague, Cheryl Taylor, approached me about re-issuing *Cow Country Cuisine*, I thought why not? Cheryl played a big part in producing the original book and has since become a successful author and publisher in her own right.

We took a hard look at the original book and discovered that one thing had not changed. Those recipes that were good in 1988, many passed down in ranching families for generations, are still just as good today. Sadly, some of the contributing cooks and ranches are no longer with us, but nonetheless we have left the recipes and attributions just as they were originally written.

In addition, we have updated the book with new recipes, including a whole section on preparing beef with a slow cooker, which has become increasingly popular. Most of the original pen and ink drawings are included, along with new photographs taken at various ranches over the past 20 years.

Americans have always loved beef, whether celebrating a special occasion or enjoying an everyday meal. Now that recent research also shows beef to be an important part of a heart-healthy diet, there's no reason not to eat it as often as you like. So turn to one of the recipes in this book and make beef for dinner tonight!

*Kathy McCraine*

## *Other Books by Kathy McCraine*

Camouflage Cuisine

ഇൻ

Mi Cocina: Traditional Mexican Cooking

ഇൻ

Cow Country Cooking: Recipes and Tales
from Northern Arizona's Historic Ranches

## *Other Books by Cheryl Taylor*
Gone to Ground

ഇൻ

## *All photos in this book shot
between 2006 and 2015 at:*

10X Ranch, Douglas, Arizona
Babbitt Ranches, Flagstaff, Arizona
Campwood Cattle Company, Prescott Arizona
Diamond A Cattle Company, Seligman, Arizona
Howard Mesa Ranch, Williams, Arizona
O'Haco Cattle Company, Winslow, Arizona
O RO Ranch, Prescott, Arizona

# ℰℭ Foreword

FROM COW COUNTRY CUISINE 1ST EDITION

It's no secret that besides the tall tales and shortcomings that come out of cow country, there's some larrupin' good recipes too. The cattle women of Arizona, joined in sisterhood as the Cowbelles since 1947, have put their "brand" of approval on this new cookbook, *Cow Country Cuisine*, along with bequeathing some tried and true recipes of their own from across the state. Our members range from rugged, country cowgirls to sophisticated city dwellers, all of whom share the same vision... to promote the cattle industry in Arizona.

As president of this dedicated group of ladies, I invite you to get out the skillet, crack open this book, and sizzle up some delectable family and crowd pleasin' cuisine.

Anne Marie Moore
1988-1989 President
Arizona State Cowbelles, Inc.


The members of the International Brangus Auxiliary are proud to be a part of *Cow Country Cuisine*. An important function of our organization is the promotion of beef as an integral part of a healthy diet, and the best advertisement for beef is a good recipe, well prepared and lovingly served.

This cookbook features the favorite recipes of those who know beef best... the producers. Try them often and with our best wishes.

Judith Wood
1988-1989 President
International Brangus Auxiliary

# ACKNOWLEDGMENTS
## FROM COW COUNTRY CUISINE 1ST EDITION

My sincere thanks to the members of the Arizona State Cowbelles and International Brangus Auxiliary for their support in producing this cookbook. Without these two groups, the book would not have been possible. I am particularly indebted to Anne Marie Moore, Judith Wood and Phyllis Taylor for their encouragement and enthusiasm.

Thanks also to my sister-in-law, nutritionist Lynne Gardner, M.S., R.D., for evaluating each and every recipe so that we could indicate those most healthful for our health conscious readers.

I owe much to my assistant, Cheryl Taylor, who did most of the production and typesetting on the book, drew the brands, and generally helped in the creative process.

Thanks also to Karen Halford, who helped proof the final book with her eagle eyes.

A special thanks to my husband, Swayze, who has critiqued my cooking for the past 12 years. He passed judgement on all the new recipes I tested for the book, and thus helped in the selective process.

And finally, a big thank you to all the cooks across the country, who shared their personal recipes to make this book a reality. What you have before you is an effort by a large group of people. Sources for recipes are indicated; where no name appears, the recipe is my own.

# ❦ TABLE OF CONTENTS

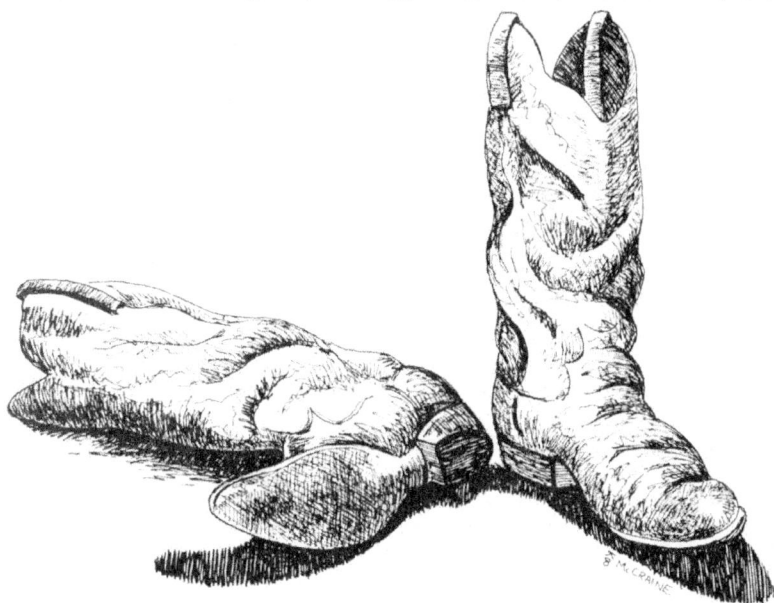

# BEEF COOKING TIMETABLES
## Timetable for Broiling

| Cut | Approx. Weight | Inches From Heat | Total Cooking Time in Min. | |
|---|---|---|---|---|
| | | | Rare | Med. |
| **Chuck Steak** | | | | |
| ¾ inch | 1 ¼ to 1 ¾ pounds | 2 to 3 | 14 | 20 |
| 1 inch | 1½ to 2½ pounds | 3 to 4 | 20 | 25 |
| 1½ inches | 2 to 4 pounds | 4 to 5 | 30 | 35 |
| **Rib Steak** | | | | |
| ¾ inch | 11 to 14 ounces | 2 to 3 | 8 | 12 |
| 1 inch | 1 to 1½ pounds | 3 to 4 | 15 | 20 |
| 1½ inches | 1½ to 2 pounds | 4 to 5 | 25 | 30 |
| **Rib Eye Steak** | | | | |
| ¾ inch | 7 to 8 ounces | 2 to 3 | 8 | 12 |
| 1 inch | 2 to 10 ounces | 3 to 4 | 15 | 20 |
| 1½ inches | 12 to 14 ounces | 4 to 5 | 25 | 30 |
| **Top Loin Steak** | | | | |
| ¾ inch | 11 to 14 ounces | 2 to 3 | 8 | 12 |
| 1 inch | 1 to 1½ pounds | 3 to 4 | 15 | 20 |
| 1½ inches | 1½ to 2 pounds | 4 to 5 | 25 | 30 |
| **Sirloin Steak** | | | | |
| ¾ inch | 1 ¼ to 1 ¾ pounds | 2 to 3 | 10 | 15 |
| 1 inch | 1½ to 3 pounds | 3 to 4 | 20 | 25 |
| 1½ inches | 2 ¼ to 4 pounds | 4 to 5 | 30 | 35 |
| **Porterhouse Steak** | | | | |
| ¾ inch | 12 to 16 ounces | 2 to 3 | 10 | 15 |
| 1 inch | 1½ to 2 pounds | 3 to 4 | 20 | 25 |
| 1½ inches | 2 to 3 pounds | 4 to 5 | 30 | 35 |
| **Tenderloin** | | | | |
| Filet Mignon | 4 to 8 ounces | 2 to 4 | 10/15 | 15/20 |
| **Ground Beef Patties** | | | | |
| ½ x 4 inches | 4 ounces | 3 to 4 | 8 | 12 |
| 1 x 4 inches | 5 1/3 ounces | 3 to 4 | 12 | 18 |
| **Top Round Steak** | | | | |
| 1 inch | 1 ¼ to 1 ¾ pounds | 3 to 4 | 20 | 30 |
| 1½ inches | 1½ to 2 pounds | 4 to 5 | 30 | 35 |
| **Flank Steak** | 1 to 1½ pounds | 2 to 3 | 12 | 14 |

# Timetable for Roasting
## (300$^0$F-350$^0$F Oven Temperature)

| Cut | Approx. Weight in Pounds | Meat Thermometer Reading | Approx.* Total Cooking Time Min. per lb. |
|---|---|---|---|
| Rib [1] | 4 to 6 | 140$^0$F (rare) | 23 to 25 |
| | | 160$^0$F (medium) | 27 to 30 |
| | | 170$^0$F (well) | 32 to 35 |
| Rib [1] | 6 to 8 | 140$^0$F (rare) | 26 to 32 |
| | | 160$^0$F (medium) | 34 to 38 |
| | | 170$^0$F (well) | 40 to 42 |
| Rib [1] (Delmonico) | 4 to 6 | 140$^0$F (rare) | 18 to 20 |
| | | 160$^0$F (medium) | 20 to 22 |
| | | 170$^0$F (well) | 22 to 24 |
| Tenderloin, whole [3] | 4 to 6 | 140$^0$F (rare) | 45 to 60 (total) |
| Tenderloin, half [3] | 2 to 3 | 140150$^0$F-170$^0$F (rare) | 45 to 50 (total) |
| Boneless Rump | 4 to 6 | 150$^0$F-170$^0$F | 25 to 30 |
| Tip | 3 ½ to 4 | 140$^0$F-170$^0$F | 30 to 35 |
| | 6 to 8 | 140$^0$F-170$^0$F | 35 to 40 |
| Top Round | 4 to 6 | 140$^0$F-170$^0$F | 25 to 30 |
| Ground Beef Loaf (9" x 5") | 1½ to 2½ | 160$^0$F-170$^0$F | 1 to 1½ hours |

*Based on meat taken directly from the refrigerator.
[1]Ribs which measure 6 to 7 inches from chine bone to tip of rib.
[2]Roast at 350$^0$F oven temperature. [3]Roast at 425$^0$F oven temperature.

# Timetable for Braising

| Cut | Approx. Weight or Thickness | Approx. Total Cooking Time |
|---|---|---|
| Blade Pot Roast | 3 to 5 pounds | 2 to 2½ hours |
| Arm Pot Roast | 3 to 5 pounds | 2½ to 3 ½ hours |
| Boneless Chuck Roast | 3 to 5 pounds | 2½ to 3 ½ hours |
| Short Ribs | 2"x 2"x 4" pieces | 1½ to 2½ hours |
| Flank Steak | 1½ to 2 pounds | 1½ to 2½ hours |
| Round Steak | ¾ to 1 inch | 1 to ½ hours |
| Swiss Steak | 1½ to 2½ inches | 2 to 3 hours |

# Beef Cuts

## AND RECOMMENDED COOKING METHODS

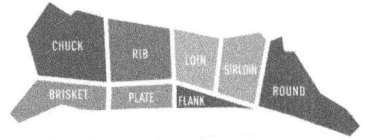

CHUCK | RIB | LOIN | SIRLOIN | ROUND
BRISKET | PLATE | FLANK | ROUND

| CHUCK | RIB | LOIN | SIRLOIN | ROUND | OTHER |
|---|---|---|---|---|---|
| Blade Chuck Roast | Ribeye Roast, Bone-In | Porterhouse Steak | Top Sirloin Steak | Top Round Steak* | Kabobs* |
| Blade Chuck Steak* | Ribeye Steak, Bone-In | T-Bone Steak | Sirloin Steak | Bottom Round Roast | Strips |
| 7-Bone Chuck Roast | Back Ribs | Strip Steak, Bone-In | Top Sirloin Petite Roast | Bottom Round Steak* | Cubed Steak |
| Chuck Center Roast | Ribeye Roast, Boneless | Strip Steak, Boneless | Top Sirloin Filet | Bottom Round Rump Roast | Stew Meat |
| Chuck Center Steak* | Ribeye Steak, Boneless | Strip Petite Roast | Coulotte Roast | Eye of Round Roast | Shank Cross Cut |
| Denver Steak | Ribeye Cap Steak | Strip Filet | Tri-Tip Roast | Eye of Round Steak* | Ground Beef and Ground Beef Patties |
| Chuck Eye Roast | Ribeye Petite Roast | Tenderloin Roast | Tri-Tip Steak | | |
| Chuck Eye Steak | Ribeye Filet | Tenderloin Filet | Petite Sirloin Steak | BRISKET | PLATE & FLANK |
| Country-Style Ribs | Short Ribs, Bone-In | | Sirloin Bavette* | Brisket Flat | Skirt Steak* |

Cross Rib Chuck Roast
Shoulder Roast
Shoulder Steak*
Ranch Steak
Flat Iron Steak
Top Blade Steak
Petite Tender Roast
Petite Tender Medallions

Brisket Point
Flank Steak*
Short Ribs, Bone-In*

### KEY TO RECOMMENDED COOKING METHODS

GRILL OR BROIL | SLOW COOKING
STIR-FRY | ROAST
SKILLET | SKILLET-TO-OVEN

* MARINATE BEFORE COOKING FOR BEST RESULTS

**BEEF**
**IT'S WHAT'S FOR DINNER.**
Funded by the Beef Checkoff.

# ℰꙅ℧ℛ℧
# BEEF AND YOUR HEALTH
## FROM COW COUNTRY CUISINE 1ST EDITION

Beef is back! After several years of taking a beating from food fad-dists, diet book authors, and even some nutritionists, beef is once again taking its rightful place in a healthy American diet.

*Fortune* magazine reports that consumers are tired of bland chicken and fish, and beef is making a comeback. "Steak and potatoes are back," says *Bazaar*. "There is nothing like the chaw of a great piece of beef... Let normal people get back to the pleasures of normal food. An article in *Self* magazine reports that "meat is one of the best health deals around, giving you more nutrition for fewer calories per bite than many other foods." One national fast food chain unapologetically proclaims their "ultimate" cheeseburger has not one, but *two* all beef patties.

Suddenly it's in to eat a *balanced* diet, one that unequivocally in-cludes beef. The reasons for this turnaround in public opinion are two-fold. One, new research is exploding the myths that point the finger at beef, blaming it for everything from heart disease to cancer. And two, modern feeding and selection methods are actually creating a product that is leaner than ever, as much as six percent less fatty than in the past.

Far from being an unwholesome product, beef is high in protein, thiamin, riboflavin, niacin, vitamin B-12, iron and zinc. Beef is what nutritionists call a "nutrient-dense" food, supplying a large share of es-sential nutrients and a relatively small share of calories. A three-ounce serving of lean beef supplies only eight percent of an adult's calorie requirements, but 45 percent of the daily protein requirements. Most people are surprised to learn that three ounces of lean roast beef con-tains 178 calories, while the same amount of baked chicken, without skin, contains 174 calories.

But what about cholesterol and beef? In the first place, the human body *needs* 1,000 milligrams of cholesterol a day, and a standard three-ounce serving of beef provides only about eight percent of that require-ment. In reality, three ounces of cooked beef contains only 73 milli-grams of cholesterol, compared to 76 milligrams for the same amount of roast chicken, 77 milligrams for pork, 130 milligrams for shrimp, and 90 milligrams for cheddar cheese.

An expert panel on high blood cholesterol sponsored by the Na-tional Heart, Lung and Blood Institute commented that, "Meat prod-ucts are rich in protein and contain iron in a form that is well absorbed; thus, meat can be included in a diet otherwise designed to lower serum cholesterol, although meat fat needs to be curtailed... It is not necessary to severely curtail the intake of red meat."

Likewise, the American Heart Association now cites the value of red meat in "heart-healthy" diets. The key word is *lean*—the meat should be trimmed of all visible fat and broiled or roasted, not fried or cooked in heavy gravy.

If you are concerned about health and diet, there are a number of steps you can take to include beef in a healthy diet:

• Always trim the fat before cooking and serving.
• Bake, broil, grill or roast on a rack, so beef will remain above drippings.
• Avoid frying. Pour off drippings when browning beef for stew, pot roast or ground beef.
• Select lean cuts of beef and extra lean ground beef. The lean cuts include eye of round, top round steak or roast, top sirloin, sirloin tips, top loin steak, tenderloin steak, and lean cubed steaks.
• Skim off the fat that accumulates at the top of soups, stews, chili or spaghetti sauces.
• Avoid gravy and cream sauces. Rely on herbs and spices for seasoning rather than butter or margarine, or heavy sauces.
• Avoid use of ready-prepared foods and mixes to avoid hidden calories.
• Marinate less tender beef cuts in spices, wine, lemon or tomato juice instead of oil; broil and slice thinly.
• Limit use of added flour, sugar or fat.

You don't have to give up beef to maintain a healthy diet. By choosing lean cuts, preparing them properly and sticking with small servings, you can dig in and enjoy America's favorite food!

———————————

*Throughout this book we have identified the recipes that are relatively low in cholesterol and saturated fat.*

*The recipes were evaluated first on cut of beef, and second on method of cooking. For instance, broiled or barbecued meats where the fat is allowed to drain away are lower in fat content than fried or stewed meats. Other ingredients also make a major contribution to fat content. Milk, cheese, eggs and cream products are very high in cholesterol and saturated fat. Saturated fat is found in both vegetable and animal sources, but is much higher in animal origin food.*

*These evaluations are intended to be used as a general guideline, and are not meant to be interpreted for self-treatment of specific diseases.*

Lynne Gardner, M.S., R.D.-1988

# STEAK

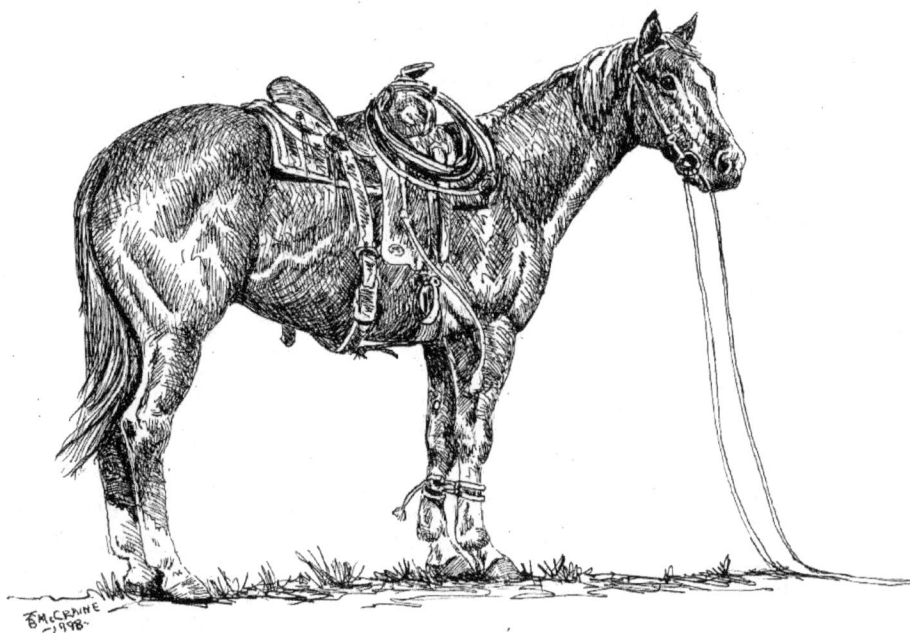

# Wild Turkey Tenderloin

*Alan and Sue Day, Lazy B Ranch, Duncan, Arizona.*

1 whole beef tenderloin
Rock salt
Black pepper
Wild Turkey whiskey

Trim the small ends off the tenderloin and roll in rock salt. Wrap in a towel and refrigerate for one week. Coat the tenderloin with pepper and marinate in the Wild Turkey for 6 hours. Grill over charcoal, turning on each side for a total time of about 30 minutes, or until done to your liking. To serve, slice across the grain.

# Surprise Steak

*Judith Wood, Wood Brangus Ranch, Dallas, Texas.*

1 Brangus sirloin steak, cut 3 inches thick
1 pound white sugar
¼ cup firmly packed brown sugar

Mix sugars together and work well into meat on all sides. Cover completely. Broil over charcoal fire for 15 minutes on each side. Place on baking sheet and bake 30 minutes at 350 degrees. The sugar will all burn off, leaving a juicy, medium rare steak.

*Good or choice grade sirloin is moderate in cholesterol and saturated fat.*

# Prosciutto Wrapped Tenderloin

4 tenderloin steaks, 1 inch thick
Salt, pepper and red pepper to taste
4 thin slices prosciutto
2 tablespoons olive oil
3 tablespoons butter
½ cup red wine
1 tablespoon bottled beef bouillon concentrate
½ cup water

Salt and pepper each steak and wrap the outer edge with the prosciutto slices, fastening with toothpicks. In a heavy skillet, heat the olive oil and 2 tablespoons of butter to medium high. Sauté the steaks about 2-3 minutes per side for rare, or until done to your liking. Remove steaks from pan and keep warm. Reduce heat and allow pan to cool slightly. Pour in wine and deglaze pan. Add bouillon and water and simmer until reduced by half. Stir in extra tablespoon of butter and melt. Pour sauce over steaks and serve. Serves 2-4.

# Chateaubriand
# With Marchand de Vin Sauce

1 whole tenderloin, about 2½ pounds
⅓ cup olive oil
Juice of 1 lemon
1 large clove garlic, crushed
Salt and coarse ground black pepper to taste
2-3 springs fresh thyme (optional)

Salt and pepper the steak and rub with a mixture of the oil, lemon juice and garlic. Let sit at room temperature about 1 hour. On a charcoal (preferably gas) grill, char the steak over an extremely hot fire, 2-3 minutes to a side. Remove steak to a roasting pan with a rack in the bottom. Bake in a preheated 375-degree oven about 20 minutes per pound for medium rare. To serve, slice thin on the diagonal, and serve with Marchand de Vin Sauce. Serves 8-10.

**Marchand de Vin Sauce:**
2 tablespoons oil
2 tablespoons flour
1 small onion, chopped fine
1 10-ounce can beef broth, plus 10 ounces water
3 tablespoons tomato paste
½ cup ham, finely chopped
½ cup chopped mushrooms
4 shallots or green onions, chopped fine
4 tablespoons butter
½ cup dry red wine
1 tablespoon lemon juice
1 tablespoon fresh chopped thyme or 1 teaspoon dried
1 tablespoon Worcestershire sauce

Make a roux by stirring 2 tablespoons oil and 2 tablespoons flour in a heavy skillet over medium heat until chocolate brown. Add onion and wilt; then add broth, water, tomato paste, ham and mushrooms. Cook until thickened and reduced to half, about 30 minutes. In a small pan, sauté the shallots in 4 tablespoons butter. Add red wine and reduce liquid by half. Add to above mixture and simmer several more minutes. Add lemon juice, Worcestershire and thyme. Before serving, strain out solids. Serve over steak.

*Good or choice grade sirloin and tenderloin is low in cholesterol and saturated fat. This recipe is low in cholesterol and saturated fat if you use unsaturated oil and low fat ham.*

# Anticuchos

1 large sirloin steak
2 garlic cloves
4-6 jalapeños
1 cup red wine vinegar
1½ cups water
2 teaspoons salt
½ teaspoon pepper
1 teaspoon oregano
1 teaspoon cumin
1 teaspoon ground red chile

In a blender or food processor, grind the jalapeños and peeled garlic to a pulp. Add all the other ingredients except the meat and mix well. Cut the meat in 1-inch cubes. Place in a large bowl and cover with marinade. Marinate overnight or all day. Place meat on skewers and cook on grill over mesquite wood, basting frequently with the sauce. Serve with warm flour tortillas and plenty of Mexican beer with lime slices.

*Good or choice grade sirloin is low in cholesterol and saturated fat. This recipe low in cholesterol and fat.*

# Four-Pepper Steaks

4 tenderloin steaks, cut 1½ inches thick
3 teaspoons Szechuan peppercorns
3 teaspoons black peppercorns
3 teaspoons green peppercorns (dried)
1 teaspoon crushed red pepper
Salt to taste
1 tablespoon olive oil
2 tablespoons butter
½ cup dry red wine
1 tablespoon bottled beef bouillon concentrate

Crush the peppers with the back of a flat wooden spoon
and mix together. Coat each of the steaks with the pepper
and salt to taste. Heat the oil and one tablespoon butter in
a heavy skillet. Sauté the steaks over medium heat for 2-3
minutes per side for medium rare. Remove the steaks and
reduce heat. Deglaze the pan with the wine and cook until
slightly reduced. Add the beef bouillon concentrate and stir.
Add 1 tablespoon butter and cook, stirring until the butter
melts and the sauce thickens. Return the steaks to the pan to
coat with the sauce and serve. Serves 4.

# Quick Peppercorn Steak

*Marion Gary, Dewey, Arizona*

4 rib-eye steaks, ¾ inch thick
2-3 tablespoons peppercorns
4 tablespoons butter
Salt to taste
¼ cup brandy
1 cup cream
¼ pound mushrooms, quartered

Crush peppercorns and press evenly into both sides of the steaks. Cover and refrigerate for several hours. Heat butter in a heavy skillet and fry steaks for approximately 3 minutes. Turn, add salt and fry for 3 more minutes. Discard the excess fat from the skillet, pour brandy over the steaks and flame. Remove steaks, add the cream and mushrooms and cook approximately 3 minutes to dissolve the juices. Pour over steaks and serve.

# Easy Chinese Steak

*Simple and good — this recipe is from Vivian L. Krentz, Phoenix, Arizona.*

2 pounds top sirloin steak
1 cup soy sauce
½ cup dry sherry
Corn starch
Oil necessary to sauté meat and vegetables
½ pound mushrooms, sliced
2 large onions, peeled and sliced

Trim steak and slice thinly across grain. Place in a glass or ceramic bowl and add ½ cup soy sauce and ½ cup dry sherry. Marinate overnight, or a minimum of 2 hours. To prepare, drain marinade from meat and pat the meat dry with paper towels. Coat well with corn starch. Heat the oil in a heavy wok or skillet until hot. Stir fry the steak in small bunches until all the meat is cooked. Drain on paper towels and keep warm. Add the onions and mushrooms to the skillet and sauté until golden brown. Return the meat to the skillet and pour the remaining ½ cup soy sauce around the edges. Heat thoroughly and stir well before serving. This is excellent served with steamed rice or cooked Chinese noodles. Also good with sautéed green beans and almonds.

*Good or choice sirloin is low in cholesterol and saturated fat. This recipe is low in cholesterol and saturated fat.*

# Sizzling Steaks and Salsa

*James Garner, actor and former spokesperson for the beef indus-*
*try's advertising campaign, was a beef eater all of his life. This was*
*one of his favorite recipes.*

1 pound boneless beef sirloin steak, cut ¾ inch thick
¾ cup chopped and seeded tomatoes
½ cup salsa
2 green onions with tops, chopped
¼ teaspoon ground cumin
½ cup finely shredded cheddar cheese
Cilantro sprigs

Combine tomatoes, salsa, onions and cumin; reserve. Trim
exterior fat and cut boneless beef top sirloin steak into 4
serving size pieces. Place each on flat surface; cover with
waxed paper and flatten with bottom of saucepan, mallet or
cleaver to ¼ inch thick. Heat nonstick frying pan over medium high heat 2 minutes. Quickly pan broil steaks 1 minute.
Turn steaks and top each with an equal amount of cheese.
Cook 1-2 minutes; do not overcook. Serve steaks over reserved salsa. Garnish with cilantro. Serves 4.

# Fajitas

*Nothing has done more to popularize skirt steak and flank steak than the invention of fajitas, which literally translates into "little sashes." Fajitas are excellent for an outdoor supper since they are a whole meal in a tortilla. Allow ⅓-½ pound of meat per person. Following are three excellent versions of this favorite.*

## Windy Acres Fajitas

Warren Wackman of Windy Acres Brangus, Brenham, Texas, is famous for his fajitas (as well as the Pina Coladas he serves with them!). Warren takes lean trimmed skirt steaks (never flank or round steak) and seasons them liberally with seasoned salt, lemon pepper and garlic salt. Then he marinates them overnight in fresh lime juice. He grills the meat quickly over hot coals and slices it diagonally against the grain. Besides the Pina Coladas, he serves it with warm flour tortillas, guacamole, sour cream, picante sauce and Pico de Gallo.

## Scooter's Fajitas

A.I. "Scooter" Robison, our partner in Twin Creek Brangus from Carencro, Louisiana, was cooking fajitas before anyone outside of South Texas knew what they were. His version calls for a flank steak sliced horizontally into ⅛-inch slices of meat. He marinates the steak overnight in a large bottle of Italian dressing, then sprinkles it with red pepper, black pepper, Worcestershire and garlic salt. He then charcoals it quickly over a hot mesquite fire. To serve, he slices the meat and serves it with warm flour tortillas, picante sauce and frijoles.

*Flank and skirt steak is low in cholesterol and saturated fat.*

# Double Duty Fajitas

*Crank up the barbecue pit once and get two, quick delicious meals with this fajita recipe from Roni White, Sasco Shorthorns, Red Rock, Arizona.*

4 pounds skirt steak
Garlic salt
Lemon Pepper
Worcestershire sauce

**Second Meal:**
2 tablespoons vegetable oil
1 red bell pepper, cut in ¼ inch strips
1 green bell pepper, cut in ¼ inch strips
1 medium onion, sliced in thin rings
¼–1 teaspoon crushed hot red pepper
¼ teaspoon dried cilantro
2 tablespoons corn starch
1 cup water

**First Meal**: Season the skirt steak to taste with garlic salt and lemon pepper. Grill over mesquite coals until done to your liking, about 5-10 minutes. Sprinkle with Worcestershire sauce as you turn the meat. For the first meal, serve half the steak with fresh salsa and warm flour tortillas. Refrigerate the remaining skirt steak for up to 3 days for the second meal.

**Second Meal:** Slice the cooked skirt steak into strips ¼ inch wide. Heat the oil in a heavy skillet, add the vegetables and sauté lightly for 2-3 minutes until heated through but still crisp. Remove the vegetables to a heated platter. Add the fajitas to the skillet and warm through. Return the vegetables to the skillet and add the cilantro and crushed hot pepper. Mix the corn starch with the water. Pour into the skillet and stir until thickened. Serve with warm flour tortillas or over hot rice. Each meal serves 4.

# Teriyaki Flank Steak

*Mrs. William Quiggle, C-Bar Ranch, Willcox, Arizona*

1 or more flank steaks
3 cups soy sauce
¼ cup fresh grated ginger
2 tablespoons minced garlic
½ cup chopped onion
3 cups sugar
1 tablespoon monosodium glutamate
3 tablespoons ketchup
1 tablespoon taco sauce
5 tablespoons honey or light corn syrup
1 tablespoon Worcestershire sauce
¼ cup sherry

Score the flank steaks. Mix the soy sauce, ginger, garlic and onion in a sauce pan and boil 5 minutes. Add the remaining ingredients and simmer at least ½ hour. Marinate the steak in the sauce for 3 hours or more. Barbecue the meat and slice across the diagonal to serve. This sauce keeps well in the refrigerator and can be used on other cuts of meat or mixed in hamburgers.

*Flank steak is low in cholesterol and saturated fat. This recipe is low in cholesterol and saturated fat.*

# Omaha Flank Steak

*Mary Kyllo, Spring Valley, Arizona*

1 flank steak
1½ cups salad oil
¾ cup soy sauce
¼ cup Worcestershire sauce
2 tablespoons dry mustard
2½ teaspoons salt
1 tablespoon black pepper
½ cup red wine vinegar
1½ teaspoons parsley
2 garlic cloves, crushed
⅓ cup fresh lemon juice

Combine marinade ingredients and marinate steak overnight. Grill over hot coals and cut steak on the diagonal to serve.

# Spicy Steak Sandwich

*This recipe from Audrey Arpin, Phoenix, Arizona was a runner-up in the 1988 Arizona Beef Cook-Off.*

1½ pounds beef flank steak, sliced thin
1 cup fresh mushrooms, sliced
2 tablespoons olive oil
2 tablespoons chopped scallions
1 tablespoon sesame oil
3 tablespoons red wine
2 teaspoons soy sauce
3 tablespoons beef stock
2 teaspoons ground Szechuan peppercorns
2 teaspoons plum jelly
6 hard rolls

Combine in a bowl all ingredients excluding beef, mushrooms, olive oil and hard rolls. Mix well. Set sauce aside. Brown beef in olive oil in a skillet or wok. Reduce heat, add mushrooms and stir fry for 10 minutes. Combine sauce with the beef mixture. Heat thoroughly for 5 minutes. Serve beef mixture on sliced hard rolls. Garnish with shredded lettuce and cold melon on skewers. Serves 6.

# A Steak in My Pocket

*This recipe by Audrey Arpin, Phoenix, Arizona, was a runner-up in the 1987 Arizona Beef Cook-Off.*

2 pounds top round steak
2 tablespoons flour
1 teaspoon basil
½ teaspoon chili powder
1 teaspoon allspice
2 tablespoons oil
1 jar (4-6 ounces) pearl onions, drained
½ cup water
¼ cup firmly packed brown sugar
1 6-ounce can tomato paste
¼ cup white wine
1 teaspoon Worcestershire sauce
1 small green bell pepper, sliced into strips
1 small red bell pepper, sliced into strips
4 pita bread pockets

Partially freeze beef. Cut into strips ¼ inch thick and 2-3 inches long. Combine flour, basil, allspice and chili powder. Dredge strips in flour mixture. Brown in oil in a large frying pan. Pour off drippings. Add onions and water to beef; cover tightly and cook slowly for 30 minutes. Sprinkle brown sugar over beef; stir in tomato paste, wine and Worcestershire sauce and cook covered for 20 minutes, stirring frequently. Add peppers and cook for 10 minutes. Cut 4 pita breads in half and fill with divided beef mixture. Stand up in bowl and serve with lettuce, sprouts, carrot curls and small celery sticks. Serves 6.

*Round steak is low in cholesterol and saturated fat. This recipe is low in cholesterol and saturated fat if you use unsaturated oil.*

# Spinach Stuffed Round Steak

*Karen Halford, executive secretary of the Barzona Breeders Association of America at Prescott, Arizona, invented this great recipe to trick her kids into eating spinach. It works best with the largest steak you can find.*

1 3- or 4-pound round steak, cut 1¼ inches thick
¼ cup red wine vinegar
1 tablespoon soy sauce
2 cloves garlic, crushed
1 small bunch fresh spinach
½ cup chopped onion
1 strip bacon, chopped
1 16-ounce box long grain and wild rice
1 tablespoon flour
Milk

Pound the round steak well until about ½ inch thick. Marinate overnight in a mixture of the red wine vinegar, soy sauce and garlic. Tear the spinach into medium size pieces and steam along with the onion and bacon about 15 minutes. Cook the rice according to directions and mix with the spinach. Let stand for several hours to blend the flavors. Sear the steak to seal its juices, then roll the spinach mixture inside the steak. Fasten with toothpicks, cover and cook in a 350-degree oven for 1½ hours, or until done, uncovering the steak for the last half hour of cooking time. Remove the steak from the pan. On top of the stove add 1 tablespoon flour to the pan juices and stir. Gradually add milk until you have a gravy of good consistency. Slice the steak in pinwheels and serve topped with the gravy.

*Round steak low in cholesterol and saturated fat. Recipe without gravy low in cholesterol and saturated fat.*

# Southern Gravy Steaks

*Martha McCraine, Woodville, Mississippi, makes the best gravy steaks in the world!*

1½ pounds round steak or seven-bone steak
¼ cup cooking oil
¼ cup flour
2 cups water
1 large onion, sliced thin
Salt and pepper

Brown the steaks in the oil in a large, heavy skillet or electric skillet. Remove steaks and add the flour, stirring until browned to a medium dark roux. Add the water and stir to make a gravy. Return the steaks to the skillet, top with the onion slices and simmer, covered, 2 hours or until tender. Add water during the cooking process if necessary to maintain a gravy consistency. Serves 4.

*Round steak low in cholesterol and saturated fat. To reduce fat in recipe, use unsaturated oil for gravy.*

# Sweet and Sour Beef

*Harold Nelson, ranch and roundup cook for the Bar T Bar Ranch at Flagstaff, Arizona, has been using this recipe since grade school. It looks complicated but is delicious and well worth the trouble.*

**Meat and Marinade:**
1 pound round steak or other lean beef, cut in 1-inch cubes
1 tablespoon good wine
2 tablespoons soy sauce
1 teaspoon fresh ginger root, or ¼ teaspoon powdered
1 clove garlic, mashed
½ teaspoon Accent
Oil for deep frying

Combine all ingredients and marinate beef overnight or at least 2-3 hours. Dip in the following batter and deep fry at 420 degrees until crisp and golden.

**Batter:**
2 egg yolks or 1 egg
Corn starch

Mix egg and corn starch together well, using enough corn starch to make a stiff batter.

**Sauce:**
6 tablespoons sugar
2 tablespoons soy sauce
1 tablespoon good wine
3 tablespoons vinegar
½ cup pineapple juice
3 tablespoons ketchup
½ cup water
3 tablespoons corn starch

Combine sugar, soy sauce, vinegar, wine, pineapple juice and ketchup in a small saucepan. Bring to a boil. Mix the corn starch in ½ cup water and stir into sauce until thickened.

**Vegetables:**
½ cup carrots, sliced thin on the diagonal
½ cup bell pepper, cut in 1-inch squares
½ cup onion, quartered
½ cup bamboo shoots, cut on the diagonal
½ cup pineapple slices, quartered
6 tablespoons oil
¼ teaspoon Accent
¼ teaspoon salt

Stir fry the vegetables in the oil with the salt and Accent for several minutes or until transparent. Add the sauce and meat. Combine well and serve.

# Beef Pepper

*Marge Perkins, Perkins Ranch, Inc., Chino Valley, Arizona*

¾ pound round steak, cut into thin strips 1 inch long
2 tablespoons soy sauce
1 teaspoon sugar
2 tablespoons corn starch
1 large tablespoon oil
1 teaspoon powdered ginger
1 green pepper, cubed
1 onion, cubed

**Gravy:**
1 teaspoon salt
1 cup water
1 tablespoon sugar
2 tablespoons corn starch
4 tablespoons soy sauce

Let the steak stand for 15 minutes in a mixture of the soy sauce, sugar and corn starch. Heat the oil in a pan and sprinkle with the ginger. Pan fry the beef, stirring quickly to medium rare and remove. Add more oil and sauté onion and pepper to crisp tender, not well done. To make gravy, mix the corn starch with the water and add remaining ingredients. Heat until thickened and add to beef, peppers and onions in a frying pan. Serve immediately over rice.

*Round steak low in cholesterol and saturated fat. Recipe low in cholesterol and saturated fat if unsaturated oil is used.*

# Bird's Nests

*Audrey Heath, Alpena, Michigan*

2 pounds boneless round steak
Salt and pepper
Dash ground cloves
1 pound bacon
1 tablespoon vinegar
1 cup water
2 bay leaves
1 medium onion, sliced thin
Crushed ginger snaps

Slice the round steak very thin horizontally. Cut in 3-inch by 4-inch pieces. Sprinkle with salt and pepper and a dash of cloves. Roll each piece of meat around a slice of bacon, cut to the same length. Secure with toothpicks and brown in a little oil. Mix the vinegar, water, bay leaves and sliced onion together and add to the meat. Simmer 2 hours. Add as many crushed ginger snaps as needed to thicken the gravy. This dish may be prepared ahead and reheated slowly in the oven before serving.

# Cornish Pasties

*Pasties (pronounced PASS-tees) originated in Cornwall, England about 1840. These "pocket pies" were brought to the upper peninsula of Michigan by Cornish miners who immigrated there to work in the iron ore mines. They would re-heat their pasties on their shovels held over the candles they wore on their hats.*

1 pound top round steak or chuck steak, cut in ¼-inch pieces
2 cups peeled and diced potatoes
2 cups diced carrots
1 cup diced onion
1 cup diced turnip
2 teaspoons salt
Pepper to taste
4 tablespoons margarine
Water
Milk

**Crust:**
3 cups flour
1 cup lard or vegetable shortening
1 egg
5 tablespoons water
1 teaspoon vinegar
1 teaspoon salt

To make crust, cut flour into shortening until crumbly. In a separate bowl, beat the egg, water, vinegar and salt together. Add to the four-shortening mixture and blend well. Divide crust into 4 parts and roll into 12-inch circles. Place ¼ of the meat, carrots, potatoes and onion on half of each circle. Sprinkle each with ¼ teaspoon salt and pepper. Dot with 1 tablespoon margarine each and sprinkle with 1 tablespoon water. Brush the edge of the pastry with water and fold in half over the filling. Seal edges and cut slits in the top. Brush with milk, place on a baking sheet and bake 1 hour at 350 degrees.

# Beef in Herbed Buttermilk

*Eloise Plants, Phoenix, Arizona, won third place in the 1987 Arizona Beef Cook-Off with this recipe.*

2 pounds beef bottom round steak, cut into 2 inch squares
    and trimmed of fat
2 tablespoons vegetable oil
3 tablespoons flour
¼ teaspoon tarragon
¼ teaspoon thyme
½ teaspoon pepper
1 large bay leaf or two small ones
2 teaspoons beef bouillon granules
1½ cups water
1½ cups buttermilk
6 medium carrots, cut into 1½ inch pieces
2 medium onions, cut into large pieces

Brown beef in oil in skillet. When browned, remove to roasting pan. Add flour, tarragon, thyme, pepper, bouillon granules, bay leaf, water and buttermilk to skillet. Stir and bring to boil, stirring to thicken. Pour over beef in pan. Add carrots and onions. Cover and bake 2 hours at 350 degrees. (If cooking liquid gets too thick, thin with small amount of water). Serve with potatoes and green salad. Serves 6.

*Bottom round steak low in cholesterol and saturated fat. Recipe low in cholesterol and saturated fat.*

# Steak Curry

2½ pounds round steak, cut into thin strips, 2 inches long
Flour for dusting
¼ cup olive oil
1 large onion, halved and sliced thin
1 cup beef broth
¼ cup red wine vinegar
3 tablespoons soy sauce
Salt and pepper to taste
3 teaspoons curry powder
2 large green bell peppers, cut in strips
1 large red bell pepper, cut in strips
4 green onions, sliced with part of the tops
1 cup piñon pine nuts (optional)

Dust steak with flour and brown in oil. Add beef broth, onion, vinegar, soy sauce, curry powder, salt and pepper. Simmer 1½ hours. Add water if sauce gets too thick. Add sliced peppers and green onions and simmer until peppers are just slightly crisp, about 30 minutes. Toast piñon nuts until slightly browned in a small skillet. Add to meat and serve over rice.

*Round steak low in cholesterol and saturated fat. Recipe low in cholesterol and saturated fat.*

# Beef Roll-Up Round Up

*Still another runner-up in the 1988 Arizona Beef Cook-Off from Marjorie Margulies, Tucson, Arizona.*

3-3 ½ pounds beef round steak, approximately 1 inch thick
¾ cup yellow corn meal
½ cup white flour, unbleached
1 teaspoon baking soda
1 egg, beaten
⅔ cup tomato juice
2 tablespoons corn oil or vegetable oil
½ cup each, green onions with tops and diced red pepper
⅓ cup each, stuffed olives and celery, chopped
2 cloves garlic, minced
½-1 teaspoon cumin
¼ teaspoon black pepper
¼-½ teaspoon salt
½ teaspoon mace

**Sauce**
½ teaspoon each, marjoram and dry mustard
1 tablespoon corn starch
½ cup beef bouillon
1 cup tomato juice
½ cup chopped pistachio nuts

Remove bone from beef. Trim fat (save to brown steak). Slit around edge to keep meat from curling. Score both sides of beef with tenderizer until beef is flattened to about ½-¾ inch thick. Render fat removed from beef and sear one side of steak. Remove from heat and place on large sheet of foil with the browned side up. Make stuffing by combining all dry ingredients. Add vegetables and spices. Stir tomato juice and corn oil into beaten egg. Mix into dry mixture. If dough is too stiff, add tomato juice until filling is spread-able. Spread filling over beef. Roll beef with filling inside.

Fasten with toothpicks. Place in a 9 x 13 inch baking dish. Combine all ingredients of sauce except pistachio nuts. Pour over round steak roll. Bake in a preheated 350-degree oven for 1 hour basting occasionally with sauce. Sprinkle pistachio nuts over meat and bake an additional ½ hour or until browned. Cut into slices. Spoon remaining sauce over slices. Serves 6-8.

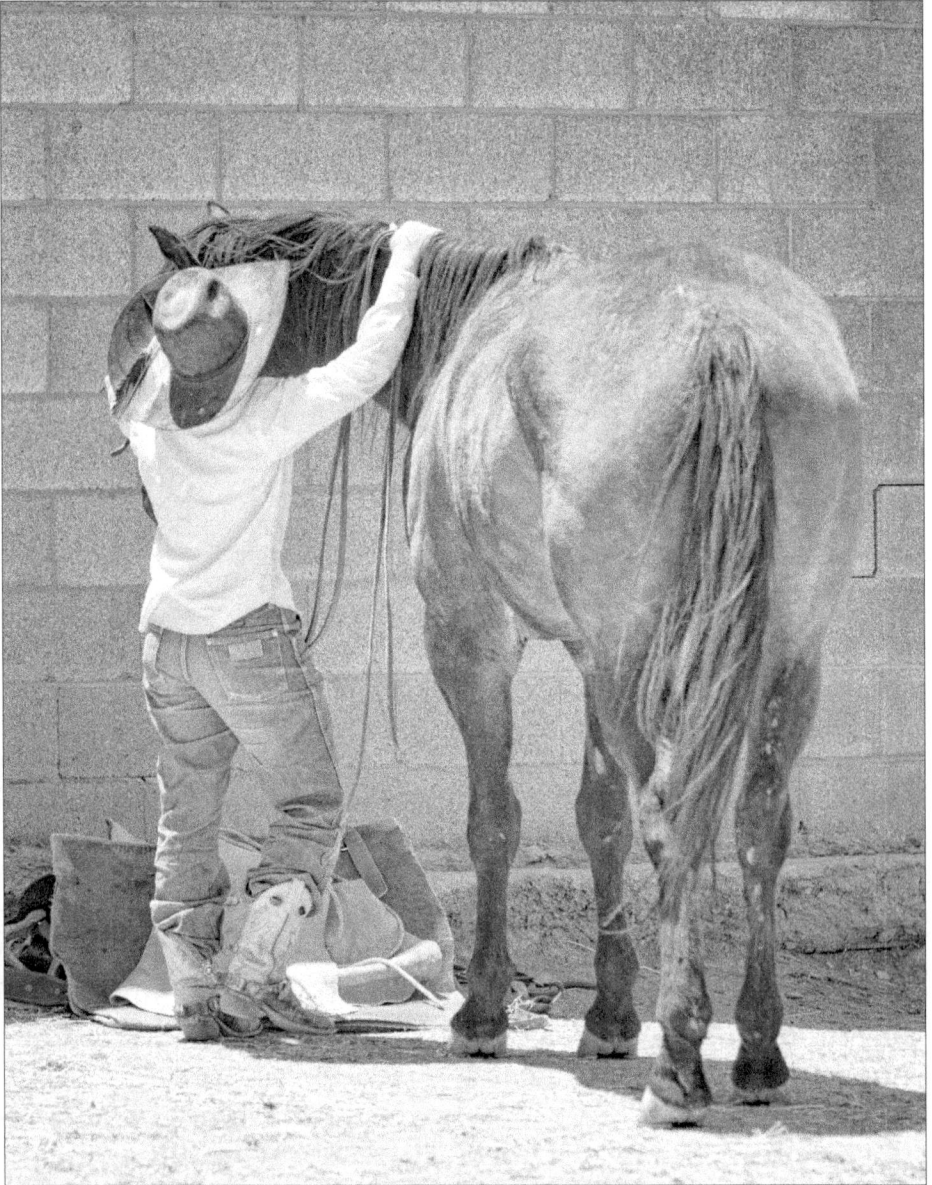

# Zesty Rolled Steak

*Ethel May O'Rear, Prescott Valley, Arizona, was the third place winner in the 1988 Arizona Beef Cook-Off with this recipe.*

1½ pounds beef round steak
¼ teaspoon salt
½ teaspoon red pepper, crushed
10 ounces frozen spinach, chopped, thawed and drained
½ cup cheddar cheese, shredded
½ cup Monterey Jack cheese, shredded
½ cup bread crumbs, unseasoned
2 teaspoons dried cilantro or parsley (save ½ teaspoon)
½ teaspoon oregano, ground
1 teaspoon vegetable oil
1 4-ounce can green chiles, diced
1 2-ounce jar pimentos, diced
¼ teaspoon salt
⅛ teaspoon black pepper
1 tablespoon vegetable oil
1 8-ounce can tomato sauce
1 cup green chile salsa
Springs of cilantro or parsley

Trim excess fat from beef and wipe with a damp towel. Place beef on cutting board and pound into a 12 x 14 inch long rectangle. Season both sides of beef with salt and red pepper. Mix together spinach, both cheeses, bread crumbs, 1½ teaspoons cilantro, oregano, oil, green chiles, pimentos, salt and pepper. With a spatula spread mixture on beef forming a layer about 4 inches wide in the center. Bring both sides of beef over filling, lapping slightly. Secure with toothpicks. Dust outside of beef roll with ½ teaspoon cilantro or parsley. Brown beef roll in 1 tablespoon oil in large skillet. Remove from skillet and place in a 9 x 13 x 2 inch baking dish. Pour tomato sauce and salsa evenly over beef roll. Cover tightly with foil and bake at 350 degrees for 30 minutes. Remove foil and cook 30 minutes. Remove foil and cook 30 minutes or until tender. Cool slightly. Cut with very sharp knife. Garnish with additional salsa and cilantro or parsley sprigs.

ॐ☯∞

# ROAST

ॐ☯∞

# Rib Roast

1 3½- pound rib roast
Salt, freshly ground black pepper, garlic powder and red
    pepper
2 large onions, sliced
1 cup water

Season the roast heavily all over with salt, freshly ground black pepper, garlic powder and red pepper. Sear over a hot mesquite fire for 3 minutes, or until browned. Meanwhile, coat the bottom of a roasting pan with the onion slices. Transfer the roast to the pan, setting it on the bed of onions. Pour in the water. Cook in a 350-degree oven for 18 minutes per pound, for rare, turning once during the cooking process. To serve, cut the ribs away from the end , and slice lengthwise. Serve with the juice and onions. Serves 4.

# Wood's Roast Beef

*Judith Wood, Wood Brangus Ranch, Dallas, Texas*

1 rump roast (or any other tender piece of beef)

Season the meat to taste. Put it into a roasting pan and cook at 500 degrees for 5 minutes per pound for rare, 6 minutes per pound for medium and 7 minutes per pound for well-done. Turn off the oven. Do not open for 2 hours. Remove and serve.

*Rump roast is moderate in saturated fat. This recipe is moderate in cholesterol and saturated fat.*

# Standing Rib Roast with Yorkshire Pudding

*Judith Wood, Wood Brangus Ranch, Dallas, Texas*

1 standing rib roast, 6½-7 pounds
Salt and pepper

Season roast well and place fat side up on a rack in a shallow roasting pan. Bake at 325 degrees for 27 minutes per pound for rare, 30 minutes per pound for medium and 35 minutes per pound for well done. Remove roast to a serving platter, reserving ¼ cup pan drippings for Yorkshire Pudding. Garnish roast with spiced crab apples, brandied peaches, and fresh parsley.

**Yorkshire Pudding:**
1 cup flour
Pinch salt
2 eggs
2 cups milk
¼ cup beef drippings

Combine flour and salt in a large mixing bowl. Add eggs and ½ cup milk. Beat with mixer on low speed until dry ingredients are moistened. Then gradually add ½ cup more milk, beating until smooth. Stir in remaining milk. Cover and refrigerate for 8 hours. Pour beef drippings in a 1½ quart, clear Pyrex baking dish and heat in a 400-degree oven until smoking, about 5 minutes. Immediately pour batter into baking dish and bake 45-50 minutes, until puffed and golden brown. Serve at once.

# Herb Crusted Steak Salad

*Sylvia Schmitt, Glendale, Arizona, was a runner-up in the 1988 Arizona Beef Cook-off with this recipe.*

2-2½ pounds beef eye of round roast
¼ cup balsamic vinegar
6 tablespoons olive oil
2 tablespoons fresh parsley, minced
2 shallots, minced
2 cloves garlic, crushed
2 teaspoons Dijon-style mustard
1 tablespoon Worcestershire sauce
2 tablespoons olive oil
1 cup dry Italian bread crumbs
1 tablespoon fresh oregano, minced
1 tablespoon fresh rosemary, finely minced
½ teaspoon garlic salt
¼ teaspoon crushed red pepper flakes
2 heads butter lettuce
1 purple onion, sliced into rings
1 7-ounce jar roasted red peppers, drained and cut julienne
3 ounces Gorgonzola cheese (or blue cheese), crumbled

Blend vinegar, oil, parsley, shallots and salt and pepper to taste in a blender until well mixed. Refrigerate. Combine and mix in a bowl: garlic, mustard, Worcestershire and oil. Rub into beef and refrigerate overnight. Combine bread crumbs, oregano, rosemary, garlic salt and pepper flakes. Roll beef in bread crumb mixture to coat. Place beef on a rack in open roasting pan in a 375-degree oven. Bake 20 minutes per pound, or until a meat thermometer reaches 135-140. Meanwhile, on a large platter, arrange lettuce leave and onion rings. Slice beef into thin slices and arrange on lettuce. Add red peppers and sprinkle with cheese. Drizzle dressing over prepared beef salad. Serves 6.

# Pot Roast Ranchera

*This recipe is great for a Mexican buffet. Before serving, shred the meat, pour a little of the juice over it and serve buffet style for filling flour tortillas. Serve extra juice with the onions and chiles. Leftover juice also makes an excellent soup stock (See Tortilla Soup recipe.)*

10 pounds chuck roast
Salt, pepper and garlic powder to taste
12 green chiles, roasted, peeled and cut in strips
3 large onions, halved and sliced thin
1 28-ounce can crushed tomatoes
2 10-ounce cans beef broth
2 cups water
4 tablespoons fresh chopped oregano, or 1 tablespoon dry

Season the meat and place in a large roasting pan. Add the rest of the ingredients and bake, covered, at 300 degrees for 4-6 hours, or until tender. Serves 16-20.

# Chalupa

*This recipe from Mary V. Waring of Waring 4/V Ranches, Flagstaff, Arizona, came from Mexico City in the 1940s. This can be prepared ahead of time and is great for a large group.*

3 pounds roast (chuck, 7-bone or blade)
1 pound dried pinto beans, washed
2 large cloves garlic, chopped
1 medium onion, chopped
2 tablespoons chili powder
1 tablespoon cumin
1 teaspoon oregano
1 4-ounce can chopped green chiles
1 29-ounce can tomatoes, cut with a knife
1 tablespoon salt, or to taste
½ teaspoon ground black pepper
Corn chips

**Garnish:**
Shredded Longhorn or Monterey Jack cheese
Chopped onions
Shredded lettuce
Sliced tomatoes
Diced avocados
Hot sauce

Put all ingredients except corn chips in a 6- or 8-quart pot. Cover with cold water and cook, covered, over low heat for 6 hours. Add hot water as needed. Remove the meat and discard bones and gristle. Cut meat into bite size pieces, return to pot and cook with lid off until thick, about 1 more hour. Serve over a bed of corn chips and top with shredded Longhorn or Monterey Jack cheese, chopped onions, shredded lettuce, sliced tomatoes, diced avocados and hot sauce. Serves 25.

# Patio Beef
*Kathy Johnson, Falls Creek Ranch, Alpena, Michigan.*

1 4- or 5-pound pot roast
1 11-ounce jar of green olives and pimentos, including juice
1 quart stewed tomatoes

Place all ingredients in a Dutch oven. Cook over medium heat until it begins to boil, then turn down heat and simmer at least 4 hours. (The longer the better.) As the meat cooks, break it apart and remove fat and bone. Stir occasionally to prevent sticking to the bottom of the pan. Note: Do not add salt as the olives flavor the meat. Serve on Kaiser buns with your favorite salad. This recipe freezes well and can be easily doubled. Always a success!

# Arizona Cashew Beef

*This recipe comes from Jewell Buechler, Fountain Hills, Arizona, and was the second place winner in the 1987 Arizona Beef Cook-Off.*

2 pounds lean, boneless chuck roast, cut into 1 inch cubes
1 tablespoon flour
4 tablespoons cooking oil
1 large onion, sliced thin
1 clove garlic, crushed
1½ cups freshly squeezed Valencia orange juice, or frozen
    concentrate
3 tablespoons freshly squeezed lemon juice
¼ cup tomato sauce
2 tablespoons soy sauce
1 tablespoon brown sugar
½ teaspoon curry powder
1 medium Valencia orange, peeled with skin removed. Cut
    into thick slices, then cut again into 6 wedge shaped pieces.
8 ounces cashew nuts, lightly toasted
1½ cups quick brown rice
1 tablespoon minced fresh parsley

Dredge beef in flour. Brown in hot oil in a large heavy skillet. Remove beef with slotted spoon to a 3-quart casserole with cover. Stir sliced onion and garlic into drippings and sauté. Spoon over beef. Mix together orange juice, lemon juice, tomato sauce, soy sauce, brown sugar and curry powder. Pour over beef mixture. Bake, covered, in a 325-degree preheated oven for 2 hours. Stir in orange wedges and cashew nuts. Continue baking for 20 minutes. Serve over hot cooked brown rice. Serves 4-6.

*Chuck is moderate in cholesterol and saturated fat. This recipe is moderate in cholesterol and saturated fat.*

# Pot Roast Indienne

*Ruth E. Anderson, Apache Junction, Arizona, won the 1988 Arizona Beef Cook-Off with this recipe.*

3-5 pounds boneless beef pot roast
½ cup peanut oil
¼ cup soy sauce
2 large yellow onions, unpeeled, coarsely chopped
2 carrots, peeled, coarsely chopped
1 tablespoon curry powder or more to taste
Salt and pepper to taste
1 cup apple juice

**Gravy:**
¼ cup flour
¼ cup cold water
½ cup plain applesauce

Rub beef with a mixture of ¼ cup peanut oil and ¼ cup soy sauce. Brown in remainder of peanut oil in heavy pan with cover. Remove beef. Lightly brown onions in pan. Sprinkle onions with curry powder (about 2 teaspoons). Add carrots and place beef, fat side up, on top of the vegetables. Add apple juice to one inch deep. Cover pan tightly and braise gently over low heat for 2½ hours, or until beef is tender. Mix flour and water together until smooth. Remove beef from pan and keep warm, letting beef rest at least 10 minutes before slicing. Strain pan juices, discarding vegetables. Thicken liquid with flour/cold water mixture, stirring constantly to eliminate lumps. Add applesauce and additional seasonings to taste and stir over medium heat until smooth and thick. Slice beef and serve on warm platter, surrounding with sauce and garnishing as desired. Serve with boiled rice and accompaniments as desired. Serves 6 or more.

# Rafter X Beef Brisket

*Anne Marie Moore of Elfrida, Arizona, also uses this recipe to marinate steaks before grilling over mesquite.*

3½ pounds beef brisket, trimmed
Liquid smoke (hickory or mesquite flavored)
Garlic powder
Onion powder
1 10-ounce bottle Worcestershire sauce
1 10-ounce bottle soy sauce

Brush brisket with liquid smoke. Rub on garlic powder and onion powder. Place in a large oven cooking bag in a roasting pan. Pour Worcestershire sauce over the meat and marinate overnight. Pierce several holes in top of bag. Roast at 325 degrees for 3½-4 hours, or until tender. Discard sauce and carve diagonally across the grain. Serves 8.

# Brisket for a Bunch

*Jeri Robson, Nuestro Hacienda, Wickenburg, Arizona*

1 5-7 pound brisket
1 16-ounce can cranberry sauce
2 packages onion soup mix
2 8-ounce cans tomato sauce
1 cup water

Place brisket in a large pan or roaster. Mix the remaining ingredients thoroughly and pour over the meat. Cover and bake at 350 degrees until tender, approximately 5-6 hours. To reheat, slice brisket thinly and heat in sauce.

# South Texas Brisket

8-10 pounds brisket, market trimmed (thin layer of fat left
    on one side)
1 10-ounce bottle Worcestershire sauce
1 to 2 tablespoons Tabasco sauce
1 stick butter or margarine
1½ cups white vinegar
1 tablespoon black pepper
2 teaspoons red pepper flakes
1 tablespoon salt
1 cup brown sugar

Place everything but brisket in a medium saucepan, bring
to a boil, and simmer 10 minutes. Marinate the meat in the
sauce at least 4 hours or overnight. Remove meat from sauce
and brown on a hot grill over mesquite chips. Place back in
the sauce in a large baking pan, cover with foil, and cook
overnight at 250 degrees. Continue cooking until meat is
fork tender. Once cooked, place meat in the refrigerator,
chill, and remove congealed fat before re-heating. (If you
can't start the meat on a grill, uncover and turn up the heat
to 350 degrees for the last hour of cooking.)

# Throckmorton Brisket

*This recipe comes from Throckmorton, Texas, by way of Mary Ma-goffin, Douglas, Arizona.*

1 5-pound brisket
2 tablespoons honey
2 tablespoons garlic powder
2 chile tepines
1 teaspoon dried oregano
1 12-ounce can or bottle of beer
Salt to taste
Parsley and cherry tomatoes for garnish

Trim as much fat as possible from the meat. Sear on all sides in a heavy pan over a burner or under the broiler. If you use the broiler, put a big piece of heavy-duty aluminum foil in a shallow roasting pan, allowing enough foil to completely cover the meat after searing, and place the meat in the middle of the foil. When the meat is a nice even brown color, remove to platter and smear a thin layer of honey on each side. Pierce the meat with a sharp kitchen fork. Poke a lot of holes in it, the more the better. Sprinkle both sides with garlic powder, then crumble the chile and oregano and sprinkle on the meat. Return to roasting pan. Add salt if you wish. Seal foil with a double fold (a hospital fold) leaving head room for steam. Before you make the final seal, add the beer, less one small sip for the cook. Seal and put in a 350-degree oven. Do not disturb for at least 3 hours; longer cooking won't hurt a thing. Carve meat in thin slices across the grain. Garnish with parsley and cherry tomatoes.

# SOUP & STEW

# Madeira Onion Soup

*This recipe is adapted from a Portuguese recipe and is much richer than its French counterpart. You could substitute dry sherry if you don't have Madeira.*

5 cups rich beef broth, preferably homemade
2 pounds yellow onions, peeled and sliced thin
2 tablespoons unsalted butter
2 tablespoons olive oil
2 whole cloves
1 teaspoon paprika
¼ teaspoon salt
¼ teaspoon fresh ground pepper
1 large egg yolk, lightly beaten
A little less than ¼ cup dry Madeira

Sauté the onions in the butter and oil in a large heavy pot over moderate heat about 30 minutes, stirring occasionally, until limp and golden brown. Don't rush this step or the soup won't have the proper onion flavor. Add the broth, cloves and paprika. Cover and simmer 1 hour, then uncover and simmer ½ hour longer. Season with salt and pepper. Mix a little of the hot soup into the beaten egg yolk, then stir into the pot and cook, stirring for 3 or 4 minutes until slightly thickened. Mix in the Madeira and serve as an appetizer or light main course.

# G'ma's Tomato Beef Soup

*Vivian L. Krentz, Krentz Ranch, Phoenix, Arizona*

2 pounds extra lean beef (stew, top sirloin or London broil),
    cubed
2-3 tablespoons oil
2 medium onions, chopped
2 large carrots, peeled and grated
2 14½ -ounce cans ready-cut tomatoes
2 10½ -ounce cans beef consommé
2 soup cans water
½ teaspoon red pepper flakes
Salt and pepper to taste
½ head (medium) cabbage, coarsely chopped
½ cup quick cooking barley

Sear meat quickly but thoroughly in a small amount of oil in
a large skillet or wok. Remove to a large soup kettle. Sauté
onions and carrots in the same skillet about 5 minutes, then
add to the meat in the kettle. Add the tomatoes, consommé,
red pepper, water, salt and pepper. Simmer on low heat 4-6
hours. One-half hour before serving add the cabbage and
barley and cook until the cabbage is tender.

*Stew beef is low in cholesterol and saturated fat. This recipe is moderate
in cholesterol and saturated fat.*

# Microwave Beef Gumbo

*Ellie Nolan, RJ Ranch, Miami, Arizona, adapted this recipe from a goose gumbo recipe that was a family favorite. To shorten the preparation time, she uses a "Tender Cooker," a pressure cooker designed for use in the microwave oven.*

2 pounds sirloin or top round, trimmed of all visible fat
1 small onion, chunked
2 garlic cloves, minced
½ teaspoon salt
¼ teaspoon cayenne pepper
¼ cup dry red wine
3 cups water

Brown the meat in a little oil in a frying pan over medium high heat. Remove to a "Tender Cooker." Add all other ingredients and cook for 20 minutes on high (600-700 watts) in the microwave oven. After cooking, let the pressure drop before opening. Cool. Strain and reserve broth. Cut the steak, which should be very tender, in bite-size pieces. (If not using a "Tender Cooker," cook the meat in a Dutch oven on top of the range for 1-1½ hours.)

**The Roux Mixture:**
⅓ cup salad oil
⅓ cup flour
1 cup chopped onion
½ cup chopped celery
¼ cup chopped bell pepper
2 cloves garlic, minced
2 tablespoons fresh parsley or 1 tablespoon dried
2 tablespoons green onions with tops, chopped

Mix the oil and flour until smooth in a 2- or 4-cup glass measure. Microwave on high for 5 minutes. Stir and microwave on high for 1 more minute. The roux should be a rich brown color, and it will be very hot. Stir in the onion, celery and bell pepper, and microwave on high for 2½ minutes. Stir in the garlic, parsley and green onions. Microwave on high for 1½ minutes.

**To Finish:**
3 cups water
¾ teaspoon salt
¼ teaspoon black pepper
½ teaspoon cayenne pepper, or more to taste

In a Dutch oven, place the broth, steak, roux mixture and all of the above ingredients. Simmer ½ hour. To serve, place a scoop of white or brown rice in a bowl and spoon gumbo over it. Serve with a tossed salad and French bread.

*Good or choice sirloin is low in cholesterol and saturated fat. This recipe is moderate in cholesterol and saturated fat if unsaturated oil is used for roux.*

# Unbelievable Soup

*Cynthia Taylor, Alpena, Michigan, named this soup "unbelievable" because she thought it was unbelievable that anything that started out looking so bad could taste so good.*

2 pounds ground beef
1 stick margarine
1 cup flour
5 cups water
1 cup onions, chopped
1 cup celery, chopped
1 cup carrots, diced
1 cup beef broth
1 teaspoon salt
½ teaspoon pepper
1 cup frozen mixed vegetables
1 16-ounce can tomatoes, chopped
4 tablespoons Worcestershire sauce
1 teaspoon garlic powder

Melt margarine in a 5-quart or larger kettle. Stir in flour and mix to a crumbly mass. Add water slowly, stirring until smooth. (A whisk works very well.) Add the onions, celery and carrots. Simmer 30 minutes, stirring occasionally. Brown the ground beef, drain and add to soup base. Add all other ingredients. Simmer 30 minutes. Serves 6-8.

# Hamburger Chowder

*Vickie Loven, Loven Brangus Ranch, Davenport, Texas*

½ pound ground chuck
1 tablespoon cooking oil
4 medium carrots, sliced (2 cups)
1 cup chopped onion
2 cups chopped celery
1 small head of cabbage, chopped
½ cup green pepper, chopped
2 16-ounce cans tomatoes, chopped
5 cups water
3 beef bouillon cubes
½ cup uncooked rice
3 teaspoons salt
1 teaspoon black pepper
1 bay leaf

Sauté beef in hot oil in a 4- or 5-quart Dutch oven until browned. Add the remaining ingredients and bring to a rolling boil. Lower heat, cover and simmer for 45 minutes or until vegetables are tender. Remove bay leaf before serving. Makes about 16 cups.

*Chuck is moderate in cholesterol and saturated fat. This recipe is moderate in cholesterol and saturated fat.*

# Beef Burgundy

*Audrey Heath, Alpena, Michigan*

2 pounds round steak, cut in 1-inch cubes
6 slices bacon, cut in 1-inch pieces
¼ cup flour
1½ cups red Burgundy or other dry red wine
1 clove garlic, chopped
1 bay leaf
1 teaspoon salt
1 teaspoon beef bouillon granules
½ teaspoon thyme
¼ teaspoon pepper
½ pound mushrooms sliced
4 medium onions, sliced
2 tablespoons margarine
Snipped parsley for garnish

Fry the bacon until crisp. Remove bacon and save for another use. Coat the beef with flour, brown in the bacon grease and drain the excess fat. Add the wine and enough water to cover the beef. Stir in the garlic, bay leaf, salt, bouillon, thyme and pepper. Bring to a boil, then reduce heat and simmer about 1½ hours, or until beef is tender. Cook and stir the onions and mushrooms in the margarine until wilted. Add to the stew and simmer 10 minutes. Thin with more water if too thick. Garnish with parsley and serve with French bread. This is also good over rice or pasta.

# Posole

*The recipe for this traditional New Mexico stew is from Jean Houston, Dallas, Texas.*

2 pounds stew meat, cut into bite-size cubes
2 cups "nixtamal" (dried hominy)
2 10-ounce cans chicken broth
3 large onions, chopped
3 garlic cloves, chopped fine
2 4-ounce cans chopped green chiles
1 16-ounce can tomatoes, chopped
Salt and pepper to taste

Soak the hominy overnight and drain. Place all ingredients in a large stew pot and bring to a boil. Simmer until tender, about 4 hours, adding water as necessary. You may use canned hominy, adding it in the last hour. This stew is traditionally served with lime slices and other garnishes, such as chopped onions, tomatoes, jalapeños and chiles.

*Stew beef is low in cholesterol and saturated fat. This recipe is low in cholesterol and saturated fat.*

# Arizona Beef Stew

2½ pounds lean stew meat, cut in cubes
3 tablespoons flour
6 tablespoons oil
1 large onion, chopped
3 large leeks with part of the green top, cut in 2-inch sections
    and quartered
2 cloves garlic, chopped fine
2 cups dry red wine
1 small can V-8 juice
1 10-ounce can beef broth, plus ½ cup water
Salt and pepper to taste
1 bay leaf
1 teaspoon dried oregano
4-5 potatoes, peeled and cubed
8 large carrots, peeled and sliced

Dust the beef with the flour and brown in the oil. Add the other ingredients, cover and simmer until done, 2-3 hours.

*Stew meat is low in cholesterol and saturated fat. This recipe is low in cholesterol and saturated fat.*

# Stew Casserole

*Betty Park, Rincon Ranch, Wickenburg, Arizona*

3 pounds lean stew meat
3 tablespoons oil
2 10-ounce cans cream of mushroom soup
½ cup dry sherry
½ package dried onion soup mix

Brown meat in oil. Add the remaining ingredients and cook in a Crockpot, or bake in a Dutch oven 2-3 hours at 325 degrees. Serves 4.

# Beef and Beer Stew

*Jerrie Burton, Seal Beach, California.*

3 cups cooked beef, cut into 1-inch cubes
2 tablespoons butter
3 large onions, peeled and quartered
8 carrots, peeled and cut in 1-inch pieces
1 clove garlic, crushed
1 bayleaf
½ teaspoon basil
¼ teaspoon thyme
2 tablespoons flour
3 tablespoons tomato paste
1 10-ounce can beef consommé or beef stock
1 12-ounce can beer
Egg noodles or rice

Melt butter in a large saucepan or Dutch oven. Add onions and cook 5 minutes to brown slightly. Add carrots, garlic and herbs and continue to cook over medium heat 10 minutes. Stir in flour, tomato paste, consommé and beer. Add cooked meat and cover. Simmer ½ hour longer, until carrots are tender and mixture is thick and aromatic. Serve over cooked egg noodles or steamed rice. Serves 6.

# Basic Beef Stock

2 pounds beef shank or other beef bones
1 large onion, unpeeled and quartered
1 large clove garlic, unpeeled and quartered
2 ribs celery
2-3 quarts cold water

Roast the beef bones and vegetables in a 350-degree oven until browned. Place all ingredients in a stock pot and bring to a boil over high heat. Then reduce heat to a gentle simmer and cook, either uncovered or with a lid set askew for 4-8 hours. The longer the cooking time, the richer the stock. Strain before using. Makes about 1 quart of stock.

ॐ

# CROCKPOT

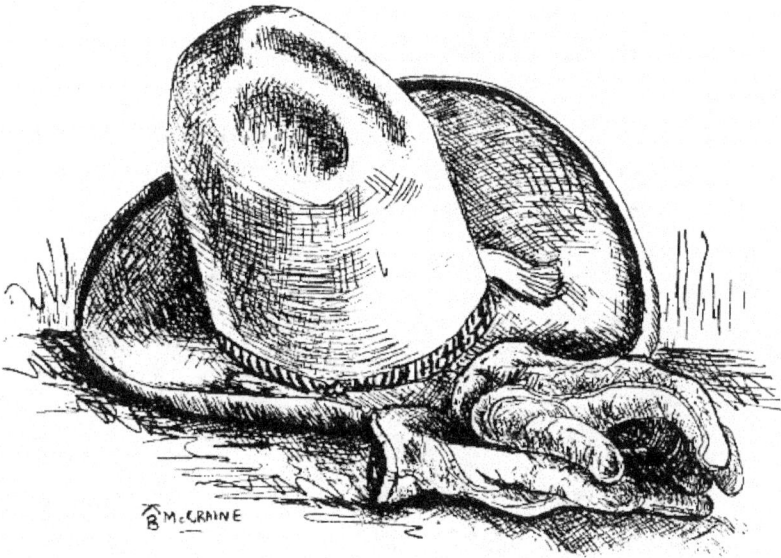

ॐ

# Slow Cooker Asian Beef

2 lbs. flank steak, sliced across the grain in 2-inch strips
½ cup cornstarch
4 tablespoons olive oil
2 onions, sliced thin
3 cloves garlic, minced
1 bunch green onions, sliced into ½ -inch pieces
1 small red pepper, sliced in thin strips
½ pound green beans, cut in 2-inch pieces
1 cup soy sauce
2 cups water
1 cup brown sugar
8 ounces hoisin sauce
1-3 tablespoons chili garlic sauce (hot)

Dredge the steak in cornstarch and shake off excess. Heat oil in a large skillet over medium-high heat. Cook the steak in batches until browned on all sides, adding oil as needed. Place in a slow cooker and stir in the remaining ingredients until well blended. Cook on high for 3-4 hours or low 6-8 hours. Serve over rice.

# Beef Bourguignonne

6 pounds beef stew meat, cut in 1-inch pieces
1-2 cups flour for dusting meat
Creole seasoning, salt and pepper to taste
¾ cup olive oil
6 thick slices of bacon, cut in 1-inch pieces
1 pound large carrots, cut in ½-inch pieces
2 large yellow onions, halved and sliced ¼ -inch thick
6 garlic cloves, minced
2 bay leaves
1 tablespoon fresh chopped thyme, or 1 teaspoon dried
1½ pounds mushrooms, halved or thickly sliced
1 bottle Pinot Noir wine
1 tablespoon concentrated beef broth
1½ cups water

Season the beef with Creole seasoning, salt, and pepper, and dredge in flour. Heat ¼ cup oil in a large sauté pan, or a 7-quart, stovetop-safe, slow cooker insert. Working in batches, brown the meat well on all sides, adding oil as needed. Remove last batch of beef from the pan and add a little more oil, the bacon, carrots, onions and garlic. Cook, stirring occasionally, about 10 minutes. Add mushrooms and continue cooking until all vegetables are soft, about 20 more minutes. Whisk in the concentrated beef broth, water, thyme, and bay leaves. Add the wine and bring to a boil, stirring to scrape up the browned bits from the pan bottom. If using the stove-safe insert, return the meat to the slow cooker, or transfer all to the cooker. Cover and cook until tender, 6 hours on high or 8 hours on low. Serve with mashed or steamed potatoes. Serves 12.

# Beef Ragu

1 5-pound brisket or chuck roast, cut in quarters
Creole seasoning
Flour for dusting
4 tablespoons olive oil
1-2 cups pancetta, cut in ¼ -inch pieces
1 large onion, chopped
6 carrots, peeled and cut in ½-inch pieces
3 fennel bulbs, sliced thin
3 cloves garlic, minced
2 pounds crimini or baby portobello mushrooms, cubed
1 28-ounce can diced tomatoes with juice
3 tablespoons chicken demi-glace
¾ 6-ounce can tomato paste
1 14-ounce can chicken broth
1¼ cups red wine
16 ounces cooked noodles

Season the beef liberally with the Creole seasoning and dust in flour. Heat the oil in a 7-quart, stovetop, cast aluminum, slow cooker insert (or separate Dutch oven if using a crockpot). Brown the beef and remove from pan. Add pancetta and cook 3-5 minutes until browned. Add onions, carrots, and fennel, and cook until wilted down, adding more oil if needed. Add garlic and mushrooms and cook down well. Add tomatoes, demi-glace, tomato paste, wine, broth, and beef. Bring to a boil and transfer to slow cooker. Cook on high for 5 hours, or low for 10 hours. Before serving, shred the beef in the pot, then serve over cooked noodles. Serves 10-12.

# Slow Cooker Stew

2½ pounds stew meat
Flour for dusting
Tony Chachere's Creole seasoning or salt and pepper
4 slices bacon, coarsely chopped
4 tablespoons oil
1 large onion, sliced
½ can tomato paste
 3 cups beef broth
¾ cup Madeira wine
1 tablespoon fresh thyme or 1 teaspoon dried
1 pound red potatoes, cut in chunks
1 pound green beans, trimmed and cut in 2-inch pieces
Salt and pepper to taste

Season meat with the Tony Chachere's, or salt and pepper, and coat with flour. Fry bacon until crisp in the stovetop-safe slow cooker insert, or separate frying pan, then remove from pan, reserving grease. Brown the meat in the bacon grease in batches, adding more oil as needed. Remove meat and sauté the onions in the grease until wilted and starting to brown. Mix tomato paste thoroughly into onions, then add the beef broth, Madeira and thyme. Transfer all to a large slow cooker and add potatoes and green beans. Add more seasoning to taste and enough water to cover. Cook on low 10-12 hours or on high for 6 hours. Serves 6.

# Pot Roast with Port

1 5-pound top round roast or chuck roast
Salt and pepper to taste
4 tablespoons olive oil
1 large onion, chopped
6 cloves garlic, minced
1½ cups Tawny Port
2 14-ounce cans beef broth
1 tablespoon fresh thyme or 1 teaspoon dried
3 bay leaves
1 pound Italian brown mushrooms, or regular button mush-
    rooms, halved or quartered

**Roux**
¼ cup oil
¼ cup flour

Season the roast with salt and pepper. Brown on all sides
in the olive oil in a stovetop-safe, slow cooker insert, or
separate frying pan. Remove the roast and add the onions.
Cook, stirring, until wilted, adding the garlic towards the
end and cooking it just until it wilts. Pour in the Port and
stir to deglaze the pan, then stir in beef broth, thyme and
bay leaves. Transfer all to the slow cooker and cook on high
for 4-5 hours, or low 8-10 hours. In a small skillet, heat the
¼ cup oil to almost smoking. Stir in the flour and reduce
heat. Cook, stirring constantly, until the roux turns a light
chocolate brown, being careful not to burn it. Add the roux
and the mushrooms to the slow cooker about 1 hour before
serving. Serve with mashed potatoes or rice. Serves 8-10.

# Busy-Day Pot Roast

1 4-pound rump roast
4 tablespoons oil
2 14-ounce cans French onion soup
1 pound small new potatoes (or more)
1 pack baby peeled carrots
1 cup water
Salt and pepper to taste

If using a stovetop-safe slow cooker insert, brown the roast in oil in the insert (or separate frying pan). Add remaining ingredients, bring to a boil and transfer to slow cooker. Cook on high for 4 hours, or low for 8 hours. If you're really short on time, just throw everything in the slow cooker and cook without browning the meat.

# Spicy Chipotle Brisket

1 7-8-pound brisket, market trimmed with thin layer of fat
Creole seasoning such as Tony Chachere's
8 garlic cloves, minced
2 onions, chopped
1 7-ounce can chipotle chilies with adobo sauce
½ cup honey
¼ cup Worcestershire sauce
4 teaspoons spicy brown mustard
¾ cup apple cider vinegar
1 tablespoon concentrated beef broth
2 bottles beer
1 teaspoon salt

For best results, season brisket well with Tony's and sear on a grill on both sides until well browned. Alternatively, sear in olive oil in a black skillet. Place chipotle chilies with sauce, honey, Worcestershire, mustard, vinegar and concentrated beef broth in a blender and blend until smooth. Add garlic and onions and pulse until blended but with some texture left in the onions. Add beer and salt and pulse just until mixed. Pour into a 7-quart slow cooker and add brisket. Cook on high 8 hours. Serves 14-16.

# ೞ೦ೞ
# CHILI

ಬೂೞ

# Chili Colorado

*It's a little more work to use real chile pulp to make chili, but you will be amazed at the difference in flavor! The best chiles are the long, dark red ones often seen strung into "ristras." They are available in most supermarkets in the Southwest or can be ordered from specialty stores. Some chile pods are hotter than others, so experiment to determine how many you want to use.*

3 pounds lean beef (chuck or shoulder), cut in small cubes
8-16 red chile pods
6 cloves garlic
2 teaspoons oregano
1 tablespoon cumin
4 tablespoons flour for dusting meat
2 onions, chopped
4 tablespoons oil
1 cup beef broth
1 can Mexican beer
Salt to taste
2-4 16-ounce cans pinto beans (optional)
1 small bunch fresh cilantro, chopped

Remove seeds and veins from the chile pods and boil slowly for 25 minutes. Remove and reserve the liquid. Using rubber gloves, slit the chiles and scrape the pulp from the tough outer skin with a dull knife. In a food processor or blender, mince the garlic, then blend in chile pulp, oregano, cumin and 1 cup of the liquid in which the chiles were boiled. Dust the beef cubes with flour and brown with the onion in oil in a large, heavy pot. Add the chile mixture, broth, beer and salt to taste. Simmer, covered, until tender, at least 2 to 3 hours. Shortly before serving stir in the cilantro and beans.

*Chuck is moderate in cholesterol and saturated fat. This recipe is moderate in cholesterol and saturated fat.*

# Chile Verde

3 pounds boneless chuck, cut in cubes
3 tablespoons flour
$\frac{1}{3}$ cup bacon grease or oil
3 onions, chopped fine
4 cloves garlic, chopped
5 cups water or beef broth
1 16-ounce can tomatoes, crushed
12 fresh green chiles, roasted, peeled and chopped
3 tablespoons fresh oregano, or 3 teaspoons dried
3 teaspoons salt or to taste
Black pepper to taste
2-3 large potatoes, peeled and cut in cubes (optional)

Dust the beef with the flour and brown in the oil in a large heavy pot. Add the remaining ingredients and simmer over low heat 3-4 hours, or until tender. Serve in a bowl with flour tortillas, or make chile burros.

# Circle Bar Chili

*Pat Taylor, Circle Bar Ranch, Foxworth, Mississippi, and Circle Bar West, Tinnie, New Mexico.*

2 pounds ground Brangus beef
1 pound lean chuck roast, cut in ¾-inch cubes
2 large onions, chopped
2 cloves garlic, finely chopped
4 tablespoons corn oil
Salt, black pepper, red pepper and white pepper to taste
2 bell peppers, finely chopped
1 16-ounce can tomatoes with green chiles, chopped
1 16-ounce can Italian tomatoes, chopped
2-3 tablespoons chili powder
V-8 juice
½ cup chicken broth made with 2-3 cubes bouillon

Sauté onions and garlic in corn oil. Add ground beef and beef cubes and sauté until lightly brown. Add salt and pepper (black, red and white). Add bell pepper and cook until softened. Add tomatoes and chiles. Add chili powder. Make chicken broth by dissolving 2-3 bouillon cubes in ½ cup water. Add broth and enough V-8 juice to make the desired liquid. Bring to low boil, cover and simmer over low heat 4-8 hours. Even better reheated and served the next day. (Red beans, if desired, should be cooked and served in a separate dish.)

*Ground beef and chuck are moderate in cholesterol and saturated fat. This recipe is moderate in cholesterol and saturated fat.*

# Stella's Chili Con Carne

*Stella Hughes of Eagle Creek Ranch, Clifton, Arizona, is the author of the popular* Chuck Wagon Cookin' *published by the University of Arizona Press. This is one of her original recipes.*

2 pounds lean beef, cubed
2 tablespoons bacon drippings
1 large onion, chopped fine
2 cloves garlic, minced
1 29-ounce can tomatoes, diced
½ cup red chili sauce or enchilada sauce.
1 heaping tablespoon red chili powder
2 cups canned, diced green chiles
½ teaspoon oregano
½ teaspoon cumin
1 tablespoon monosodium glutamate
½ cup vinegar
1 rounded tablespoon brown sugar
Salt and pepper to taste
Water

Cut the meat into bite-size pieces. (Do no use hamburger.) Brown meat in a heavy iron skillet or Dutch oven in bacon drippings or lard. When beef is nicely browned, add all other ingredients. Cook over low heat until very tender. Let cook down, adding hot water, a little at a time to keep from sticking. Do not add thickening. When cool, this chili con carne can be rolled in large flour tortillas and frozen. Serves 6.

*This recipe is moderate in cholesterol and unsaturated fat.*

# Chili For A Chew

*Randa Wakefield, Double Diamond Brangus, Forgan, Oklahoma.*

1 pound ground beef
1 pound dried pinto beans
3 teaspoons salt
4 tablespoons oil or bacon drippings
1½ cups chopped onions
2 cloves garlic, minced
¼ teaspoon black pepper
1 8-ounce can tomato sauce
1 28-ounce can tomatoes
½ cup raisins
2 ribs celery, sliced
2 tablespoons chili powder

Add beans to 6 cups warm water in a 5- or 6-quart pot and let stand overnight. Do not drain. Add 2 teaspoons salt, cover and boil gently over low heat. While beans are cooking, heat the oil or bacon drippings in a 12-inch skillet. Add the onions and sauté for 5 minutes over low hat. Add beef and garlic and cook until beef is browned. Add 1 teaspoon salt, pepper, tomato sauce, tomatoes (undrained), raisins, celery and chili powder. Add the beef mixture to the beans, cover and cook 2 hours. Serve with fresh cornbread or muffins. Serves 6 hearty appetites.

*Ground beef is moderate in cholesterol and saturated fat. This recipe is moderate in cholesterol and saturated fat is unsaturated oil is used.*

# Red Wine Chili

3 pounds ground beef
2 large onions, sliced
6 tablespoons shortening or oil
2 bell peppers, chopped
1 28-ounce can tomatoes, chopped
6 cloves garlic, minced
3 teaspoons salt
6 whole cloves
2 bay leaves
6 tablespoons chili powder, and more to taste
2 4-ounce cans green chiles, chopped
Chopped jalapeños to taste
1 16-ounce can red kidney beans, drained
2 16-ounce cans pinto beans, drained
1 cup dry red table wine (not cooking wine)
Fresh chopped cilantro to taste

Brown the onion in oil. Add the beef, garlic and bell pepper. Brown, stirring as the meat cooks. Drain off grease. Add the tomatoes, salt, cloves, bay leaves, chiles, jalapeños and chili powder. Cover and simmer at least 2 hours. Add the beans and wine. Simmer until heated through. Add fresh chopped cilantro before serving. Serve with Mexican cornbread or flour tortillas.

# Cincinnati Chili

*Robin Darrow, Phoenix, Arizona*

2 pounds lean ground beef
4 cups beef broth or water
2-4 cups finely chopped onions
1-1½ tablespoons minced garlic or 1-1½ teaspoons garlic powder
1 teaspoon to ¼ cup chili powder
1 teaspoon to 4 tablespoons cinnamon
1-2 teaspoons crushed pepper
2-4 teaspoons cumin
1 teaspoon salt
1-2 teaspoons allspice
½-1 teaspoon ground cloves
1-3 bay leaves
2 tablespoons cider or vinegar
2 tablespoons Worcestershire sauce
1 6-ounce can tomato paste
½ ounce unsweetened chocolate

In a large pot boil the ground beef, beef broth and onions. Simmer one hour. Add remaining ingredients (Cincinnati Chili is meant to have more of a cinnamon flavor than a spicy flavor, so use your own judgement on the seasoning.) Simmer 1-3 hours until the desired consistency is achieved. Remove fat and serve. This chili is served 5 ways:

1-Way Chili: Chili only
2-Way Chili: Chili over spaghetti
3-Way Chili: Chili over spaghetti, topped with shredded cheese.
4-Way Chili: Chili over spaghetti, topped with shredded cheese and chopped onions.
5-Way Chili: Chili over spaghetti, topped with shredded cheese, onions and kidney beans.

# GROUND BEEF

# Beef Eggplant Casserole

*This original recipe from Dorothy Fisher, Sonoita, Arizona, is very Italian and very good.*

1 pound ground beef
1 large eggplant, peeled and cut in slices lengthwise
Seasoned flour
1 egg, beaten
4-5 tablespoons olive oil
1 large onion, chopped
3-4 cups spaghetti sauce
1 pound ricotta cheese
½ pound mozzarella cheese, shredded

Soak the eggplant in salted water to eliminate bitterness. Dip eggplant slices in seasoned flour, then the egg, then the flour again to coat well. Heat the olive oil in a large heavy skillet and sauté the eggplant on both sides until browned. Remove the eggplant and set aside. In the same skillet brown the ground beef and onion together. Line the bottom of a 9 x 13 inch casserole with some of your favorite spaghetti sauce. Fold the eggplant slices around the meat taco style and place in the casserole in a single layer. Add the ricotta cheese on top of that, followed by the mozzarella cheese. Pour the rest of the spaghetti sauce over the whole dish and bake about 1 hour at 350 degrees. Great served with spaghetti. Serves 6-8.

*Ground beef is moderate in cholesterol and saturated fat. This recipe is moderate in cholesterol and saturated fat if you use only egg white for the batter.*

# German Stuffed Cabbage Rolls

*Judith Wood, Wood Brangus, Dallas, Texas*

1 pound ground beef
1 large head cabbage
2 onions, sliced
1 8-ounce can tomato sauce
4 tablespoons brown sugar
5 tablespoons lemon juice
8 gingersnaps, crushed
Paprika, ketchup, salt and pepper to taste
1 small onion, minced
⅛ cup raw rice
Salt and pepper

Parboil cabbage 5 minutes. Remove large leaves, remove veins and lay flat. Simmer sliced onions, tomato sauce, sugar, lemon juice, gingersnaps and seasonings until blended. Mix meat, minced onion, rice, salt and pepper and divide onto cabbage leaves, 2-3 tablespoons per leaf. Fold sides in first, then roll. Place loose side down in a heavy pan, cover with sauce and bake at 250 degrees for 1½ hours. Check for dryness and add liquid if necessary.

*Ground beef is moderate in cholesterol and saturated fat. This recipe is moderate in cholesterol and saturated fat.*

# Overstuffed Hamburgers

*It takes one whopper of an appetite to consume one of these in one sitting, but don't make the mistake of trying to reduce the size or you won't be able to get enough stuffing in. This recipe from Cheryl Taylor, Dewey, Arizona, is fun to do for a group, letting everyone choose his own combination of stuffing ingredients.*

½ pound ground beef per person
Garlic salt, onion salt and black pepper to taste

Divide the meat into quarter-pound balls and place half the balls on pieces of tin foil. Flatten the balls with the palm of your hand and place a piece of plastic wrap on top. With a rolling pin, roll each out to ⅛-inch thick. Remove the plastic wrap and mound the stuffing in the center of the meat. Roll the other half of the balls out the same way, then drape over the stuffing. Roll up the edges and seal into a large hamburger. Wrap with the tin foil and slash a few small holes to allow the grease to drain. Cook on the charcoal grill over low heat until done to your liking.

**Stuffings:**

| | |
|---|---|
| Cheddar cheese | Mozzarella cheese |
| Blue cheese | Mushrooms |
| Onions | Green onion |
| Tomatoes | Green chiles |
| Bell peppers | Jalapeños |
| Celery | Garlic |

Shred the cheese and chop all the other ingredients, placing each in a separate dish. Let each person choose his own combination of ingredients for the stuffing.

# Spanish Rice Skillet

*Dorothy Miller, Tolleson, Arizona*

1½ pounds ground beef
6 slices bacon
1 cup rice, uncooked
1 large onion, chopped
¼ cup green pepper, chopped
1 16-ounce can stewed tomatoes
1½ cups water
2½ teaspoons chili powder
½ teaspoon salt
¼ teaspoon pepper

Cook bacon until crisp in a 12-inch skillet; remove bacon and brown the rice. Add and brown the beef and onion. Add rest of ingredients, stir and simmer, covered, for 35 minutes. Crumble bacon on top. Serves 6.

# Crown C Burgers

*The late Jane Carrington of the Crown C Ranch, Sonoita, Arizona, dreamed up the original version of this recipe, and used it for the community dances during the 1940s and 1950s. Peggy Monzingo of ZR Hereford Ranch, Benson, Arizona, uses it today to serve crowds, multiplying the ingredients as needed. The recipe makes either hamburger patties or meatballs to serve over rice or pasta.*

**Beef Patties:**
1 pound ground beef (preferably chuck)
1 small onion, minced
2 slices fresh white bread, shredded
¼ cup cream or canned milk
¼ teaspoon each, salt, pepper, cumin and ginger
2 tablespoons ketchup
1 teaspoon Worcestershire sauce
2 tablespoons lemon juice

**The Sauce:**
¼ cup ketchup
½ can beef consommé
½ teaspoon celery seed
½ teaspoon ground mustard
½ cup water
¼ cup tomato paste
2 tablespoons brown sugar
2 tablespoons medium hot salsa

Combine patty ingredients thoroughly and shape into patties or meatballs. Broil until just brown, turning once. (Or fry in a skillet if preferred.) Place in a casserole or slow cooker. Combine sauce ingredients and add to meat. Bring to a simmer to heat thoroughly and finish cooking meat. The broiled meat may be frozen and reheated in the sauce. Five times the recipe will serve about 25 hamburgers or make 60 medium size meatballs.

# Beef Picadillo Dip

*Catherine Simpson, Tallman Brangus Farms, Dibble, Oklahoma.*

1 pound ground Brangus beef
2 tomatoes, diced
1 small onion, chopped
¾ cup chopped pimento
¾ cup silvered, toasted almonds
1 teaspoon salt
1 teaspoon pepper
2 cloves garlic, finely minced
½ teaspoon oregano
½ cup seedless white raisins
¾ cup water
10 ounces chopped ripe olives
3 ounces canned, chopped mushrooms
1 10-ounce can tomatoes and green chiles

Brown beef in a heavy skillet. Add remaining ingredients, cover and simmer for two hours. Serve hot with corn chips or tostados. Serves 10-12.

# Stuffed Beef Meatballs in Sherry Sauce

*This recipe from Gerald Bacon, Munds Park, Arizona, was the winning recipe in the 1987 Arizona Beef Cook-Off.*

2 pounds lean ground beef
1 4-ounce can diced green chiles
1 egg
1 medium onion, finely diced
2 cloves garlic, minced
2 tablespoons parsley flakes
20 small mushroom caps, up to 1 inch in diameter, stems removed, washed and drained
2 ounces blue cheese, crumbled into ¼ -½ inch pieces
2 tablespoons olive oil

Place beef in large mixing bowl; add chiles, onion, garlic, parsley and egg. Mix well. Let stand 30 minutes to allow flavor to blend.

**Sherry Sauce:**
1 6-ounce can tomato paste
1 8-ounce can tomato sauce
¾ cup dry white wine (or water)
2 tablespoons onion, finely diced
1 clove garlic, minced
1 tablespoon Worcestershire sauce
¼ cup rice wine vinegar
1 teaspoon paprika
2 teaspoons dry mustard
⅓-½ cup sherry (or Cognac if preferred)

Mix ingredients thoroughly in a 2-quart saucepan, bring to boil, cover and simmer for 25-30 minutes. Prepare meatballs using beef mixture (approximately 1½ ounces). Pat beef flat between palms making a patty 2-3 inches round. Spoon 1 teaspoon of sherry sauce on each patty. Place 1 mushroom cap, stem side up, on sauce; place one or two pieces of blue cheese inside mushroom cavity. Fold edges of patty up over ingredients and seal by forming a meatball. Heat olive oil in skillet on medium heat and add meatballs, browning on all sides. As meatballs brown, drop gently into sherry sauce and cook for 30 minutes. Spoon sauce over meatballs to ensure all are cooked in sauce. Serve with potatoes and salad, or over pasta or rice. Serve remaining sauce in bowl. Serves 6-8.

# Chinese Meatballs

*Carrie Drumlevitch, Tucson, Arizona, was a runnerup in the 1987*
*Arizona Beef Cook-Off with this recipe.*

1 pound lean ground beef
3-4 teaspoons soy sauce
1 tablespoons dry sherry
1 tablespoon beef broth or water
1 large green onion, finely chopped (including green top)
1 teaspoon fresh ginger root, finely minced, or ⅛ teaspoon
    ground ginger.
10 grindings black pepper
1 small clove garlic, pressed or 1/16 teaspoon garlic powder
½ tablespoon corn starch
1 egg, lightly beaten
8 medium water chestnuts, finely chopped
½ teaspoon vegetable oil

**The Sauce:**
2 teaspoons corn starch
½ cup beef broth defatted, (dilute according to directions, if
    canned)
1 teaspoon soy sauce
⅛ teaspoon sugar (optional)

Combine in bowl: soy sauce, sherry, beef broth, green onion, ginger, pepper, garlic, corn starch and egg. Stir well.
Add beef and water chestnuts and mix well. Form mixture
into 12 meatballs. Preheat vegetable oil in nonstick pan over
high heat for 1 minute. Lower heat, add meatballs to pan
and brown until cooked. Cover and remove pan from heat.
Combine well the last 4 ingredients in saucepan. Over medium heat stir constantly until sauce thickens and clears. Simmer sauce for one minute over low heat. Drain meatballs on
paper towel. Serve meatballs and gravy over rice or Chinese
noodles. Serves 3-4.

# Italian Meat Roll

*Instead of ordinary meat loaf, grace your table with this meat loaf in disguise from Judith Wood, Wood Brangus, Dallas, Texas*

2 pounds very lean ground beef
2 eggs, beaten
¾ cup fresh bread crumbs
½ cup tomato juice
2 tablespoons minced parsley
2 cloves garlic, minced
½ teaspoon dried oregano
Salt and pepper to taste
8 slices boiled ham
6 ounces shredded mozzarella cheese
3 slices mozzarella cheese, sliced diagonally

Combine the beef with the next 7 ingredients. Mix well with a fork. On waxed paper, pat beef mixture out into a 12 x 10 inch rectangle. Place ham slices on meat and sprinkle with shredded cheese. Carefully roll meat, beginning at short end and using the paper to lift the meat. Moisten the edges and ends of meat and seal. Place roll, seam side down, in a 9 x 13 baking pan. Refrigerate until ready and bake at 350 degrees for 1 hour and 15 minutes. Place cheese wedges over meat and bake 5 more minutes until cheese melts. Serve with a colorful marinated vegetable salad.

*Ground beef is moderate in saturated fat. This recipe is moderately high in cholesterol and saturated fat.*

# Chili Beef Casserole

*Connie Dotson, Wheat Belt Brangus, Enid, Oklahoma.*

1½ pounds ground beef
½ cup chopped onion
⅓ cup chopped green pepper
¼ cup chopped celery
⅛ teaspoon garlic powder
2 tablespoons shortening
2 8-ounce cans tomato sauce
1 16-ounce can kidney beans
2-3 teaspoons chili powder
1-1½ teaspoons salt

**Topping:**
½ cup all-purpose flour
½ cup cornmeal
1 tablespoon sugar
2 teaspoons baking powder
1 egg
½ cup milk
2 tablespoons shortening

Sauté the onion, green pepper, celery and garlic powder in the shortening. Add beef and cook until browned. Drain off excess grease. Add tomato sauce, kidney beans, chili powder and salt. Simmer 5-10 minutes. Pour into a 2-quart baking dish. To make topping, sift flour, cornmeal, sugar, and baking powder together. Combine egg, milk and shortening. Add to dry ingredients and stir until smooth. Spread over beef mixture and bake at 400 degrees for 15-20 minutes. Serves 6.

# Barbecued Beans and Beef

*A simple but good one-dish meal from Kitty Cashion, Flint Brangus, Woodbury, Georgia.*

1 pound ground beef
6 slices bacon, cut into pieces
1 medium onion, chopped
2 16-ounce cans pork and beans
¾ cup brown sugar
1 teaspoon Worcestershire sauce
1 tablespoon mustard
½ cup ketchup

Brown the ground beef with the bacon pieces and onion in a large skillet. Remove the meat from the skillet and add the beans, brown sugar, Worcestershire sauce, mustard and ketchup. Stir and heat until well blended and hot. Mix with the meat and pour into a greased casserole. Bake at 325 degrees for one hour or until cooked through.

# Beef 'n Bacon Turnovers

*Julia Cox, Sault Ste. Marie, Michigan.*

1½ pounds ground beef
1 medium onion, chopped
1 tablespoon shortening
6 slices bacon, diced
2 tablespoons flour
1 teaspoon salt
½ teaspoon pepper
1 10-ounce can cream of mushroom soup
1 cup sour cream

**The Crust:**
1 egg
1 pound lard or shortening
6 cups flour
4 teaspoons salt
1 teaspoon baking powder

**Crust:** Beat the egg and add water to make 1 cup. Use usual pastry directions, cutting shortening into flour, then stirring in water and egg mixture.

**Filling:** Brown the onion in shortening. Add the ground beef, bacon, salt, pepper and flour. Cook until done and drain all the fat. Stir in the soup, cover and simmer 20 minutes. Stir in the sour cream and simmer 5 minutes. Set aside to cool.

**The Assembly:** Use a coffee can lid as a cutter for large turnovers, or a biscuit cutter for hors d'oeuvres. Roll the crust as for a pie crust and cut into desired size. Wet the edges, fold in half and fill. Press the edges with fork tines to seal and prick with a fork before baking. Bake at 425 degrees for 10-

20 minutes, depending on size, until light brown. These can be frozen after assembly. To bake frozen turnovers, extend cooking time by 5-10 minutes.

# Greek Yourvarlakia
*Judith Wood, Wood Brangus, Dallas, Texas.*

1 pound ground round
½ cup cooked rice
1 tablespoon each, chopped onion and parsley
½ tablespoon hot water
½ teaspoon crushed dried mint
1 small egg, lightly beaten
¾ teaspoon salt
Pinch of allspice and cinnamon
12 cherry tomatoes

**Avgolemone Sauce:**
3 large eggs
1 tablespoon corn starch
½ cup fresh lemon juice (2 lemons)
1 cup beef bouillon

Mix the first eight ingredients together well, shape into 12 2½-inch balls, and dust with flour. Chill. Thread onto skewers, alternating with cherry tomatoes. Bake at 350 degrees for 30-35 minutes. While kabobs are baking, prepare the Avgolemone Sauce by beating eggs until foamy. Add corn starch and lemon juice in a saucepan over low heat. Slowly add hot bouillon, stirring constantly until sauce thickens and coats spoon, about 8 minutes. Top kabobs with sauce just before serving. Rice is the usual accompaniment.

# Bar-B-Q Beef Patties

*Dorothy Bixby, Bixby Ranch, Globe, Arizona*

2 pounds ground beef
1 teaspoon salt
Dash of pepper
1 small can tomato soup
¼ cup sweet pickle relish
¼ cup chopped onion
1 tablespoon brown sugar
1 tablespoon Worcestershire sauce

Mix ground beef, salt and pepper. Form patties and brown in skillet. Pour off fat. Combine remaining ingredients and pour over patties. Simmer about 20 minutes, stirring occasionally. Makes 8 good size patties.

*Ground beef is moderate in cholesterol and saturated fat. This recipe is moderate in cholesterol and saturated fat.*

# Surprise Meat Loaf

*Erin Boss, Douglas, Arizona.*

1½ pounds lean ground beef
1 cup tomato soup
1 teaspoon salt
Dash of pepper
1 small onion, chopped
1 cup crushed cracker crumbs
1 egg beaten
2 hard-boiled eggs

Combine all ingredients except boiled eggs. Peel eggs and form loaf around them. Place in a loaf pan and bake for 1 hour at 350 degrees. Serves 6-8.

# My Favorite Meat Loaf

1½ pounds ground beef
½ bell pepper, chopped
1 small onion, chopped
1 egg, slightly beaten
½-¾ cup bread crumbs
½ cup ketchup
¼ cup milk
Salt, pepper and Worcestershire sauce to taste
1 16-ounce can crushed tomatoes
½ cup stuffed green olives, sliced
1 2-ounce can rolled fillets of anchovies with capers

Mix everything together except tomatoes, anchovies and olives. Kneed well and shape into loaf in an oblong baking dish. Top with the tomatoes, sliced olives and anchovy rolls, and bake at 350 degrees for about 1 hour.

# Spaghetti Sauce

*Val Riggs, C Bar Ranch, Willcox, Arizona.*

5 pounds lean ground beef
1 teaspoon thyme
1 teaspoon oregano powder
3 tablespoons oregano leaves
3 cloves garlic
1 teaspoon marjoram
1 medium onion, chopped
1 6-ounce can black olives (chopped if desired)
1 teaspoon cumin
1 15-ounce can tomato sauce
4 quarts canned tomatoes
2 6-ounce cans tomato paste
1 tablespoon basil
Salt and pepper to taste

Brown meat in a 6-quart kettle. Drain, add remaining ingredients and simmer for at least 2 hours. Serve over spaghetti, topped with Parmesan cheese. Serves 25, or freezes well for later use.

# Spaghetti and Meatballs

*Jerri Burton, Seal Beach, California.*

2 pounds ground round
½ of a 9-ounce box bread crumbs
1 egg
Garlic powder to taste
1 cup finely chopped celery
1½ cups grated Romano cheese
Salt, pepper and sugar to taste

**The Sauce:**
1 6-ounce can tomato paste
4 16-ounce cans tomato sauce
8 cups water
1 cup chopped celery
½ cup dried onions
2 cloves garlic, chopped
½ cup dried onions
2 cloves garlic, chopped
½ cup dried parsley
2 tablespoons oregano
2 tablespoons Accent
1 tablespoon anise seed
3 tablespoons olive oil
4 tablespoons sugar
Salt and pepper to taste

Mix meatball ingredients and form into 1-inch balls. Combine sauce ingredients in a large saucepan, bring to boil and simmer several hours until thick. Add meatballs after the first hour. You may also add sweet and hot Italian sausage.

# Hamburger Steaks in White Wine Sauce

1½ pounds lean ground beef
4 tablespoons fresh crushed black pepper
Salt to taste
2 tablespoons butter
6 small green onions sliced with half of tops
½ cup dry white wine
½ cup crushed tomatoes with puree
1 tablespoon fresh cilantro, chopped

Divide the hamburger meat into 4 patties. Press the pepper into both sides of each and sprinkle with salt to taste. Cook in a medium hot skillet about 5 minutes per side, or until just pink inside. Remove patties, lower heat and add the butter. Sauté the green onions in the butter about 2 minutes until wilted. Add the white wine and deglaze the pan. Add the tomatoes and cilantro and stir. Add the patties back to the sauce and cook just long enough to heat everything. Serve the sauce over the meat. Serves 4.

*Ground beef is moderate in cholesterol and saturated fat. Use unsaturated oil or margarine to reduce fat in recipe.*

# Mexican Cornbread

*Sam Hudson, Silsbee, Texas.*

1-1½ pounds ground beef
1 medium onion, chopped
2 tablespoons bacon drippings or oil
1 cup cornmeal
1 cup milk
1 egg
½ teaspoon baking soda
Pinch salt
1 16-ounce can cream style-corn
1 cup shredded cheddar cheese
3 or 4 jalapeño peppers, chopped

Brown meat and onions and drain well. Put cast iron skillet, with bacon drippings or oil, in oven to preheat. Combine cornmeal, baking soda, salt, egg, milk and corn. Pour half of the batter into the skillet, then add meat, onions, cheese and peppers. Top with the remainder of the batter. Bake at 375 degrees for 45 minutes, or until well browned.

# Beef and Potato Cakes

*Stella Hughes, Eagle Creek, Ranch, Clifton, Arizona.*

2 cups cooked beef, ground
2 cups mashed potatoes
2 eggs
1 small onion, minced
½ cup tomato juice
1 teaspoon salt
Pepper to taste

Combine meat, mashed potatoes, eggs, onion, tomato juice and seasonings. Shape into 8 patties, place in a greased baking dish and brush with melted butter. Bake at 350 degrees for 30 minutes.

# Ground Beef Hash

*Pearl Willis, Duncan, Arizona.*

1½ pounds ground beef
½ cup diced onion
3 tablespoons flour
4 or 5 grated potatoes
1 teaspoon salt
¼ teaspoon pepper
2 or 3 cups water

Cook ground beef and onion in a 12-inch heavy skillet until meat loses its pink color. Sprinkle flour over meat and onion mixture and mix thoroughly. Add grated potatoes and salt and pepper. Cover with water and stir. Simmer until potatoes are done, stirring frequently and adding water if needed.

# Border Casserole

*Katherine Gary, Dallas, Texas.*

1½ pounds ground beef
3 tablespoons salad oil
¾ cup chopped onion
1 clove garlic, minced
1½ tablespoons chili powder
2 tablespoons paprika
½ teaspoon oregano
1½ teaspoons salt
1½ teaspoons pepper
2½ cups tomato puree
3 cups cooked kidney beans
1 cup crushed corn chips
1 cup American cheese, shredded

Brown beef in oil. Add onion and garlic and cook 5 minutes. Stir in chili powder, paprika, salt, pepper, oregano, tomato puree, beans and corn chips. Pour into a greased casserole. Top with shredded cheese and bake 50 minutes at 350 degrees.

# Chili Cheese Dip

*Jolene Miller, Goodyear, Arizona.*

2 pounds ground beef
1 large onion, chopped
1 8-ounce can green chile salsa
1 16-ounce can refried beans
1 10-ounce can chili beef soup
½ teaspoon garlic salt
¼ teaspoon chili powder
Salt and pepper to taste

**Topping:**
2 cups shredded Longhorn or cheddar cheese
¼ cup chopped green onion tops
1 16-ounce can black olives, diced
Corn or tortilla chips for dipping

Brown beef and onion and drain. Add salsa, beans, soup and seasonings, mix well and simmer 30 minutes. Top with cheese, green onion and olives. Serve hot with chips for dipping.

# Green Enchiladas

*Vickie Loven, Loven Brangus Ranch, Deport, Texas.*

1 pound ground beef
1 medium onion, chopped
1 7-ounce can chopped green chiles (hot or mild)
1 pound American cheese
1 10-ounce can cream of chicken soup
1 cup milk
½ cup water
12 corn tortilla shells

In a large skillet, sauté the ground beef and onions until browned. Add the green chiles. In a double boiler, melt the cheese, then add soup, milk and water. Cook briefly, then combine with beef mixture and stir well. Layer 4 tortilla shells in the bottom of a sheet cake pan and spread with half the beef mixture. Make another layer of shells and top with the remaining beef mixture. Top with the remaining shells. Bake for 20-25 minutes at 375 degrees and let sit 5 minutes before serving. This dish is best when leftover.

# Italian Goulash

*Cynthia Taylor, Alpena, Michigan.*

1 pound ground beef
1 cup macaroni
1 cup onions, diced
1 clove garlic, minced
1 8-ounce can tomato sauce
½ teaspoon salt
½ teaspoon pepper
1 cup ketchup
1 8-ounce can mushrooms or 1 cup fresh sliced mushrooms
2 tablespoons Worcestershire sauce
1 teaspoon Italian seasoning

Cook macaroni and drain. Brown ground beef, onion and garlic. Add all other ingredients and simmer 5 minutes. Add macaroni and simmer an additional 5 minutes.

# BARBECUING FOR A CROWD

# Uncle Lesley's Barbecued Beef

*Lesley Flowers, Baton Rouge Angus breeder and retired county agent with Louisiana State University's Extension Service, is a man with over 25 years experience cooking beef. Barbecue is his speciality, and he's cooked for hundreds of local and state organizations in Louisiana. He likes to use an inside round steak or whole round filet trimmed of all excess fat, "so I don't have to trim it off the sauce later." The meat is cooked in pans in a large, outdoor barbecue oven. The fire, preferably of pecan wood or other hardwood, is built in the lower part of the oven, underneath a wire mesh on which the pans of meat are set to cook. The same recipe would work in a conventional oven, but you would not get the same smoked flavor.*

15 pounds steak
26 ounces ketchup
3-4 ounces wine vinegar
12 ounces cider vinegar
3 ounces Worcestershire sauce
3 ounces A-1 Sauce
1 ounce black pepper
1½ ounces salt
3-4 ounces brown sugar
1 tablespoon celery seed
1 tablespoon allspice
1 pound onions, chopped
½ ounce Bouquet
1 ounce chili powder

If using a barbecue oven, start the fire about 30 minutes ahead and cook down to coals. Continue to add wood as needed. Mix all ingredients except the chili powder. Dip the meat in a small pan of vinegar and then the sauce. Place the meat in a shallow pan and then pour the sauce over it.

Cook, uncovered, over a slow fire for 2-3 hours, turning the meat every 20-30 minutes. Sprinkle the chili powder over the sauce while it cooks.

*This recipe is low in cholesterol and saturated fat if good or choice grade round steak is used.*

# Mr. Steiney's Louisiana Barbecue

*Lesley Flowers, who developed the preceding barbecue, originally learned to barbecue from the late Albert Steinbach of Baton Rouge. "Mr. Steiney" as he was called is still referred to as "the barbecue king" around Baton Rouge. This is his original recipe, which was also cooked in an outdoor barbecue oven.*

150 pounds beef of your choice
1 gallon apple cider vinegar
1 quart wine vinegar
8 ounces black pepper
2 gallons ketchup
2 10-ounce bottles Worcestershire sauce
2 10-ounce bottles A-1 Sauce
3 ounces celery seed
3 ounces allspice
24 ounces salt
10 pounds onions, chopped
1 pound brown sugar
1 16-ounce bottle Italian or French dressing or combination
    of both
1 quart mustard
2 tablespoons red pepper

Mix all the ingredients together. Dip the meat in vinegar, then in the sauce. Sprinkle chili powder over the meat, place in a large shallow pan and cover with the sauce. Cook in the oven on medium heat 2-3 hours, turning the meat every 30 minutes. Serves 250.

# Los Alamos Barbecue

*According to the folks around Los Alamos, California, this famous barbecue method originated in the 1920s with the area's old timers, most of whom were of Swiss-Italian descent. The nearby town of Santa Maria adopted the method and claimed it for their own, but don't ever call it "Santa Maria Barbecue" around Al Monighetti of Los Alamos. He was there when the old timers started the Los Alamos Barbecue, and he knows his history! Today he carries on the tradition by cooking for all the big events in the area. I had the opportunity to try his barbecue at an annual meeting of the Barzona Breeders Association of America. Unlike most barbecued meat, Al's is served medium rare, but nevertheless, it is so tender it melts in your mouth. Following are the ingredients and the general instructions for barbecuing. The amounts will depend on how big a crowd you are feeding.*

Several "tri-tip" roasts (a 4- or 5-pound roast from the tip of
    the sirloin)
Salt and pepper
Garlic salt

For a big group Al cooks on a large, brick, above-ground pit that measures 3 feet high, 4 or 5 feet wide and 10 feet long. He starts by building a big fire of live oak or red oak wood in the pit. He lets the fire burn, adding wood as necessary, for an hour and a half, until it burns down to coals. He seasons the meat well with salt, pepper and garlic salt, then skewers it on steel rods long enough to lie across the top of the pit. Then he lays the skewered meat across the top fat side up. The meat cooks a total of 45-50 minutes for rare or 1 hour and 15 minutes for well done. Halfway through the cooking process he turns the meat fat side down. The trick is to sear the meat fast and keep the juices in. A conventional screen or grate barbecue pit can be used instead of the rods, but it is the oak wood that gives the barbecue its flavor. Serve with Los Alamos Pinquito Beans and Salsa.

**Salsa:**
6 medium tomatoes, diced
2 medium onions, diced
2 cloves garlic, minced
1 8-ounce can diced green chiles
Salt to taste

Mix all ingredients in a bowl, cover and chill overnight.

*Good or choice sirloin is low in cholesterol and saturated fat. This recipe is low in cholesterol and saturated fat.*

# Horner Mountain Ranch Pit Barbecue

*In Arizona the most popular method of barbecuing meat for a crowd is the deep pit barbecue. At Horner Mountain Ranch near Dugas, Arizona, we put on a pit barbecue every spring after roundup for about 125 friends and neighbors. Every cook in Arizona has his own ideas about how to season and wrap the meat for the pit— ours is a little different than any I've seen.*

*In Mexico where the pulque Maguey grows prolifically, they line their pits with the juice-filled fleshy leaves or "pencas" of the ma-guey plant to impart a unique and exquisite flavor to the meat. In northern Arizona our maguey, or "mescal" plant (also called the century plant) grows much smaller, the leaves only reaching 12-14 inches in length. Instead of lining the pit with them, we wrap the meat in the leaves for the same effect.*

**Preparing the Pit:**
The first thing you have to do is dig a pit. Ours is 4 feet deep and about 3 feet in diameter. We placed some rocks on the bottom and then set a 30-inch long section of round culvert in the hole. The culvert isn't really necessary, but it makes the pit more permanent for use every year. We filled in around the culvert with more malapai rocks to help hold the heat in. About 4 hours before the meat is to go on, the night before the barbecue, we build a big fire in the pit, us-ing any hardwood available—mesquite, oak or fruit wood. We keep the fire going until we have 10 inches of hot coals on the bottom. Then we're ready to add the meat.

**Preparing the Meat:**
The first step in getting the meat ready for the pit is to cut the mescal leaves. We roast these over a charcoal fire until they begin to soften and split. Then we split them horizon-tally so that we have two, thinner, more pliable leaves.

We use 15-pound chuck roasts, and can fit about 80 pounds in our pit, figuring on ½ pound of meat per serving. We season the meat heavily — very heavily-with salt, garlic powder, onion powder, black pepper and red pepper. Then we wrap the mescal leaves round the meat, cut side in, and wrap it all in heavy foil. Next we place the meat in wet burlap sacks and attach a piece of bailing wire to make it easier to retrieve the bundle from the pit after it is cooked.

When the fire is ready, around 10 or 11 o'clock in the evening, we throw enough dirt on the coals to just cover them and stack the meat on top of that. We cover the hole with a piece of tin and shovel 6 or more inches of dirt over the whole thing. It is imperative that there be no air holes and no smoke escaping from the hole. After that you can go to bed, party, or whatever, and forget about the whole thing. In 12-18 hours you will have the tenderest meat you ever tasted. My dad, who first showed us how to do this, says you could cook an old bull by this method and it would still be tender.

We serve the meat with Rosa Cordova's homemade flour tortillas, frijoles and a choice of barbecue sauce or picante sauce.

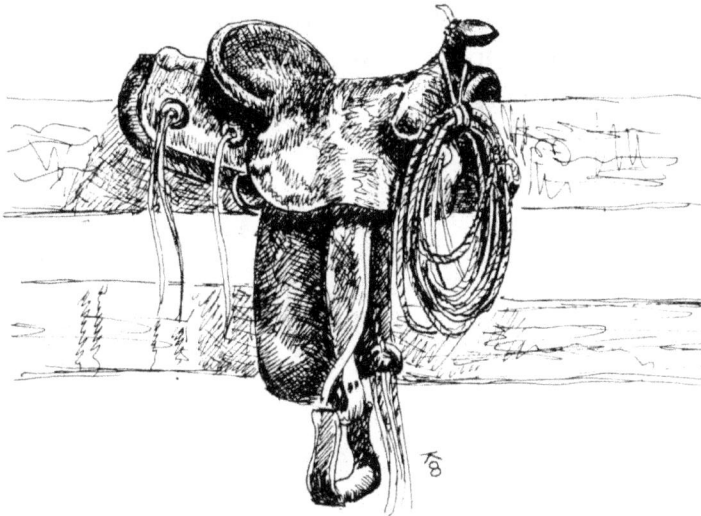

# Sidney's Twin Creek Barbecue

*When we lived in Mississippi, we used to put on a 4th of July barbe-cue every year at our Twin Creek Brangus Ranch near Centreville. In addition to feeding about 200 people, we had match horse rac-ing, cutting, barrel racing and a big barn dance. Sidney Haggart made himself famous around there for the way he could cook meat, and he usually made an all-night affair of it with plenty of beer for anyone with the stamina to keep up with him.*

Several large roasts, about 12-15 pounds each
Onion salt
Garlic salt
Red pepper
Black pepper

Sidney always seasoned the meat heavily and let it sit with the seasoning overnight. He had a giant barbecue pit made out of a barrel, and in this he would build a fire at one end. He started out by searing the meat over the fire, then he would place it on the grill at the opposite side from the fire. He smoked the meat there about 6 hours, turning and bast-ing occasionally with oil. After 6 hours, he would remove it from the pit and wrap it in foil. He continued to cook the wrapped meat on the grill 4 more hours, or until time for the barbecue to start. Once wrapped, the meat can stay on the grill any length of time.

# Garth's Barbecue Seasoning Mix

*Here is still another pit recipe from Garth Lunt of Arroyo Seco Brangus Ranch at Pima, Arizona. He serves his with a good barbecue sauce, cabbage salad, beans and Dutch oven biscuits.*

100 pounds beef
5 pounds sugar
1½ pounds salt
4 ounces dry mustard
2 ounces black pepper
2 ounces cayenne pepper
1 gallon vinegar (or as needed for mixing)

Mix ingredients together to form a smooth paste. Have meat cut in 10-12 pound chunks. Cut deep slashes a few inches apart and rub seasoning mix into cuts and all over the outside of the meat. Wrap in pieces of old sheets and put enough wrapped chunks of meat in a wet burlap sack to fill half way. Fold over the top half of the sack and place, folded side down, on an 18-inch bed of mesquite or oak coals, in a pit 4 feet deep. Cover immediately with sheet iron and sufficient dirt to seal off all air (approximately 12 inches of dirt.) Cook 10-12 hours, depending on the amount of meat you have in the pit.

# Cowman's Barbecue Sauce

*Stella Hughes, Eagle Creek Ranch, Clifton, Arizona, wrangled this recipe from a man who ran a popular barbecue stand in Claypool, Arizona, back in the late 1940s*

1 cup beef stock (made from neck meat with plenty of tallow attached)
1 cup vinegar
1 cup ketchup
Juice of 1 lemon
1 8-ounce can tomato sauce or tomato paste
3 large onions diced
1 clove garlic, minced
½ cup brown sugar
1 cup water
1 tablespoon liquid smoke
1 tablespoon red chili powder
2 teaspoons sugar
1 teaspoon black pepper
1½ teaspoons salt
½ teaspoon cloves

Mix all ingredients and simmer at least 1 hour. Longer is better. Serve on roast, ribs, steaks or beefburgers. Leftovers can be frozen. Makes about 6 cups of sauce.

# ෨෪

# THIS & THAT

෨෪

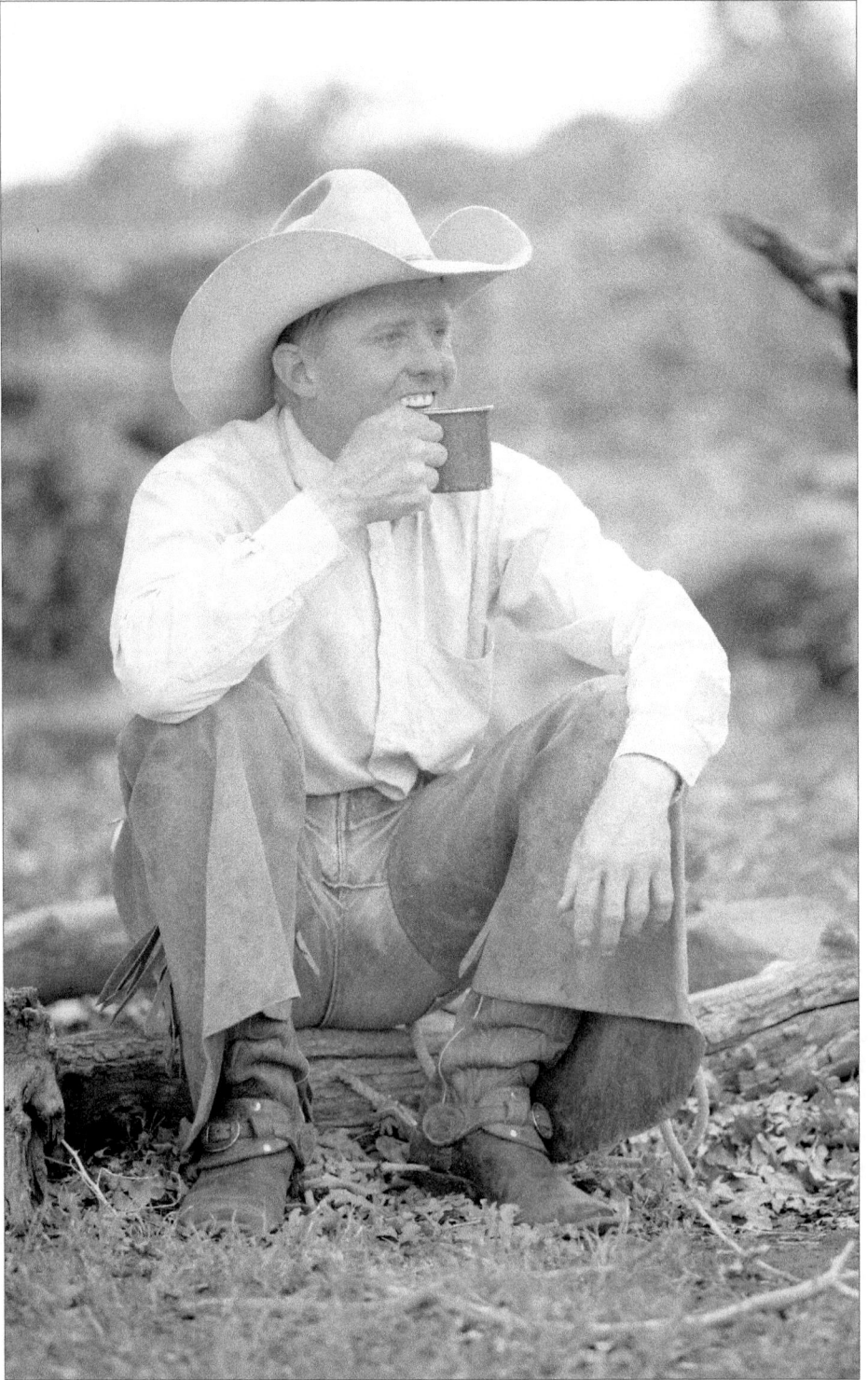

# Portly Ribs

*This runner-up in the 1987 Arizona Beef Cook-Off comes from Shirley Murch, Tucson, Arizona.*

3 tablespoons vegetable oil
1½ pounds boned short ribs of beef
3 tablespoons olive oil
3 cloves garlic, finely sliced
2 medium onions, sliced
3 tablespoons flour
1 cup beef broth
1 cup water
½ cup Rhine wine
2 tablespoons tomato paste
6 juniper berries, crushed
1½ teaspoons paprika
1½ teaspoons sugar
1 teaspoon salt
½ teaspoon pepper
½ cup Tawny Port wine
2 tablespoons parsley, chopped
8-10 sprigs parsley

In a large frying pan, heat oil over high heat. Add boned short ribs of beef and quickly brown on all sides. Remove to a paper towel to drain. In a 5-quart Dutch oven, heat the olive oil over high heat. Add garlic and onions. Cook, stirring to sauté the onions. Lower heat to medium and stir in the flour. Cook, stirring 2-3 minutes. Add stock, water, Rhine wine, tomato paste, juniper berries, paprika, sugar, salt and pepper. Stir to mix. Add in boned short ribs. Cover with lid. Bring to a boil over high heat. Lower heat and simmer 1½ to 2 hours until beef is tender. Remove beef to heated platter (with a well) with a slotted spoon and keep warm. Add Port wine to gravy. Cook 3-5 minutes to reduce slightly and to blend flavors. Pour gravy over beef. Garnish beef with parsley. Serves 4.

# Sweet and Sour Ribs

*Tammy Ogilvie, Ogilvie Cattle Company, Flagstaff, Arizona, got this recipe from her grandmother, Mrs. Charles McKinney of the Bar CL Ranch at Pearce, Arizona. It's best with very lean ribs.*

2½-3 pounds short ribs
Flour
Salt and pepper to taste
3-4 tablespoons shortening
1 cup sliced onions
1 clove garlic, chopped fine
1 small bay leaf
⅓ cup ketchup
¼ cup vinegar
1½ cups hot water
3 tablespoons brown sugar

Cut ribs into individual pieces and trim excess fat. Roll in flour and season with salt and pepper. Brown well on all sides in a large skillet in the shortening. Remove to a Dutch oven. Add onions and garlic to the pan drippings and sauté until lightly browned. Add to the ribs. Combine all other ingredients and add to the ribs. Cover and cook 2½-3 hours. To thicken sauce, remove ¾ to 1 cup of liquid from the ribs and place in a small saucepan. Add 2 tablespoons flour, bring to a boil and cook until thickened. Pour over ribs and serve with rice or noodles.

# Barbecued Short Ribs

*Peggy Boss, Douglas, Arizona*

2½ pounds beef short ribs, cut into serving size
1 large onion, sliced

**Barbecue Sauce:**
1 cup tomato ketchup
1 cup water
1 teaspoon chili powder
2 tablespoons vinegar
2 tablespoons Worcestershire sauce
1 teaspoon paprika
1 teaspoon salt (optional)
½ teaspoon pepper
1 teaspoon sugar

Brown ribs a few at a time in a large heavy (cast iron) frying pan. Put the ribs in a large shallow roaster with a tight fitting lid. Cover with the onion slices. Combine the barbecue sauce ingredients and simmer for 15 minutes. Pour over ribs and cover tightly. Bake at 325 degrees for 1½-2 hours. Baste occasionally. Serves 4.

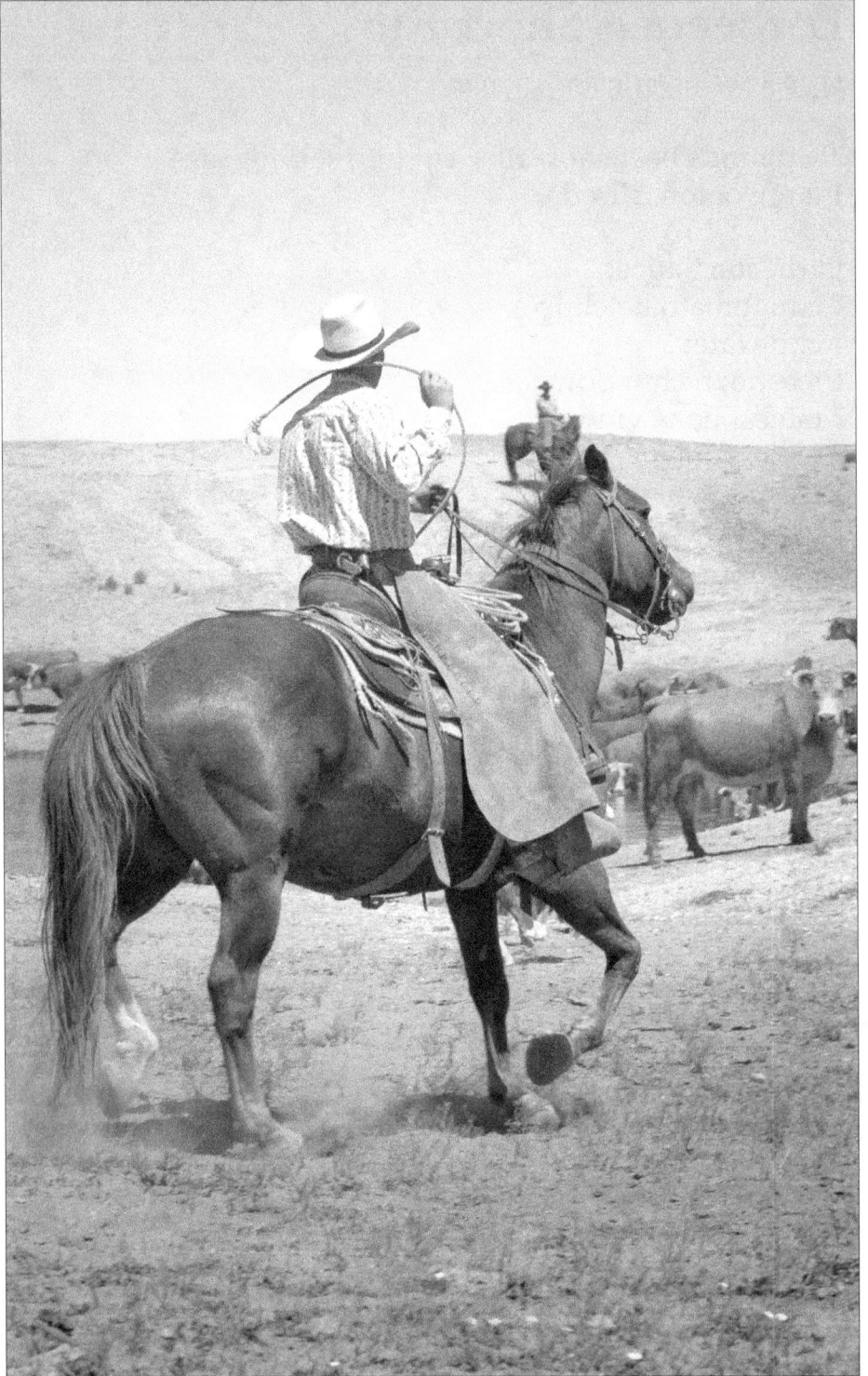

# Curried Beef Ribs

6 pounds beef ribs
½ cup soy sauce
4 tablespoons brown sugar
2 tablespoons curry powder
4 dried hot peppers
8 cloves garlic
1 teaspoon black pepper
4 tablespoons oil

Place all ingredients except the ribs in a blender and blend to a fine sauce. Marinate the ribs in the sauce for 2 hours or more. Sear over high heat on the grill, then move the ribs to the side of the grill off the fire and cook slowly for 1 hour or until done. Turn and baste with the sauce several times while cooking. Serves 6.

# Deviled Rib Bones

*Judith Wood, Wood Brangus Ranch, Dallas, Texas*

Roasted rib bones
Salt and pepper
English mustard (dry)
Cream
Bread crumbs
¼ cup melted butter

Take freshly roasted rib bones and trim them, leaving a generous amount of meat on them. Sprinkle with salt and pepper. Make a thin paste of dry mustard and cream. Coat the ribs with mustard paste. Sprinkle generously with bread crumbs, covering bones completely. Drizzle with butter and broil until crusty, turning to crisp on all sides.

# Pillowcase Jerky

*Alan and Sue Day of the Lazy B Ranch at Duncan, Arizona, contributed this recipe. Alan says he occasionally likes to add extra seasoning, such as seasoned pepper, cayenne or garlic power. But he really prefers it just the way the old cowboys made it–"Salt, pepper and fly specks."*

1 large boneless butt
Salt and pepper

Cut the individual muscles out of the meat, then cut off and discard all the fat and connecting tissue. Cut the meat across the grain very thin, 1/16 to ⅛ of an inch. The thinner the slices, the easier it will be to dry. Salt and pepper the meat generously on both sides, using more pepper than salt. Lay out the meat strips on a cake rack or oven rack without overlapping them. Set the rack in an insert fireplace, and cook on low heat for 8-10 hours, turning every 3-4 hours, until dried. You can do the same with a dehydrator or oven, but it won't turn out as good. After it's done, store in a pillowcase. Don't store in plastic, as the meat has to be able to breath, and a paper sack will leave a paper taste.

*This recipe is moderate in cholesterol and saturated fat.*

# Beef Jerky

*Cynthia Taylor, Alpena, Michigan.*

2-3 pounds round steak, chuck steak or chuck roast
1 teaspoon onion salt
½ teaspoon salt
½ teaspoon garlic salt
½ teaspoon lemon pepper
½ teaspoon sausage seasoning
½ teaspoon thyme
½ teaspoon oregano
½ teaspoon marjoram
½ teaspoon basil

Combine spices in a dish. Cut meat into strips less than ¼ of an inch thick. Remove ALL fat. Sprinkle one side with the combined seasonings and beat with a meat hammer. Turn and repeat seasoning and beating. Place the strips on a cookie sheet or other flat pan. Place in a 120-degree oven for 4 hours. Turn and put back for another 4 hours. Keep the oven door propped open for the entire time to allow moisture to escape. With a gas oven the pilot light may be enough to provide the heat. Store in a plastic bag.

*Round steak is moderate in cholesterol and saturated fat. This recipe is moderate in cholesterol and saturated fat.*

# Cowbelle Tea Sandwiches

*This recipe came from a Cowbelle in Fremont County, Wyoming, by way of Louise Cook, Cook Ranch, Tubac, Arizona. It is a delicious, different addition for parties or receptions.*

½ cup dried beef, chopped
1 8-ounce package cream cheese, softened
2 tablespoons blue cheese, crumbled
⅓ cup chopped walnuts
2 teaspoons minced onion tops
4-5 drops Tabasco sauce
⅛ teaspoon cayenne pepper
Approximately 10 slices whole wheat bread

Whip cheese and add rest of ingredients. Spread on slices of whole wheat bread with crusts removed. Freeze overnight, or chill thoroughly before cutting into squares.

# Homemade Corned Beef

*Jolene Miller, Goodyear, Arizona*

1 4-5 pound brisket
1½ cups coarse salt (not iodized)
½ ounce saltpeter (available in some drug stores)
2 tablespoons brown sugar
3 bay leaves
3 tablespoons pickling spices
6 cloves garlic, slivered

Combine 4 quarts of water, salts, sugar, bay leaves, and pickling spices. Boil 5 minutes, then cool. Place beef in a large glass or stoneware crock. Add liquid mixture, slivered garlic, and more water if needed to cover meat. Place a heavy plate over meat and add weight to keep meat submerged. Tie muslin over top of crock and let stand in a cool place 2 weeks. During warm weather place in the refrigerator.

**Preparing For Cooking:**
2 bay leaves, whole
1 clove minced garlic
1 quartered onion
10 peppercorns
¼ cup vinegar

When ready to cook, rinse the meat and place in Dutch oven. Add fresh water to cover and add all the above ingredients. Bring to boil and simmer until meat is tender, 3-4 hours or cook 1½ hours in a pressure cooker.

# Machaca and Eggs

*Dr. Ray Rodriguez of Tucson, Arizona, is fortunate to have many friends in Mexico through his dealings in cattle and veterinary supplies. They frequently present him with gifts of gorditas (small, fat flour tortillas) and machaca. The machaca is made by hanging the meat and drying it as jerky. Then it is shredded with a stone "molcajete." The following recipe is a joint effort from Ray and Sheri Holbrook, also of Tucson. It makes a great Sunday breakfast.*

2 cups dried machaca
2-3 tablespoons oil
1 onion, sliced thin
2 green chiles, roasted and sliced, or 1 4-ounce can
1 large tomato, chopped
½ bottle beer
Scrambled eggs

Sauté the machaca, onion, chiles, and tomato in the oil, moistening with the beer. Cook about 15 minutes, or until vegetables are done. Serve with the scrambled eggs, picante sauce and gorditas or flour tortillas.

# Heart in Tomato Sauce

*Katherine Groseta, W Dart Ranch, Cottonwood, Arizona.*

1 beef heart
½-1 teaspoon salt
1½ tablespoons shortening
1 onion, chopped
1 garlic clove, minced
1 or 2 8-ounce cans tomato sauce
1 large bay leaf
2 tablespoons minced parsley
Cooked rice

Cut out coarse fibers on top and inside of heart. Wash in cold water. In a large pot, cover with water and add ½-1 teaspoon salt. Simmer, covered, until tender, 1½-2 hours, depending on size of heart. When done, but in cubes. To make sauce, melt 1½ tablespoons shortening in a large skillet. Add chopped onion and garlic and cook until lightly browned. Add one or two 8-ounce cans of tomato sauce, depending on the size of the heart. Stir in cubed heart, the bay leaf and the parsley. Simmer slowly for ½ hour and serve over cooked rice.

# Braised Beef Shanks

4 beef shanks, cross cut about 1 inch thick
2-3 tablespoons oil
1 large onion, chopped
2 cloves garlic, minced
½ cup red wine
4 medium size potatoes, sliced
1 cup beef broth
1 16-ounce can tomatoes, chopped
Half of a 4-ounce can of chopped green chiles

Brown the shanks in oil. Remove and add onions and garlic. Cook until slightly browned, then add ½ cup red wine and deglaze pan. Cook about 2 minutes. Place shanks in a baking dish, scatter potatoes on and around them, and pour the wine mixture over all. Add beef broth, tomatoes and chiles. Cover and bake about 6 hours at 275 degrees. Remove the cover for the last hour of cooking.

# Oldtime Rancher's Mincemeat

*Stella Hughes, Eagle Creek Ranch, Clifton, Arizona.*

2 calves' tongues, boiled until tender (approximately 2 hours)
Rind and juice of 2 oranges
Rind and juice of 2 lemons
2 pounds of sugar
1 pound raisins
1 pound currants
¼ pound citron
3 pounds tart apples, chopped
1½ pounds chopped suet
1 tablespoon salt
1 pint brandy
2 pints good whiskey
½ teaspoon each of cloves, nutmeg and cinnamon

Peel and trim the cooked calves' tongues, and put through a meat grinder with the 2 oranges and 2 lemons. Add sugar, raisins, currants and citron. Mix well. Chop apples (do not peel), and add to meat. Add spices, suet, salt, brandy and whiskey. Mix well. Put into a crock and cover with cloth. Place in a cool room for at least four weeks. When making pies, if mixture is too thick, moisten with orange juice or more brandy.

# Curtis Mincemeat

*This 100-year-old recipe was passed down to Marge Perkins of the Perkins Ranch, Inc. at Chino Valley, Arizona, from her sister, Erna Curtis. It originated with Christine Curtis, who homesteaded the Walker area of Arizona in 1900.*

5 cups chopped beef
1½ cups chopped suet
15 cups chopped apples
5 cups sugar
2½ cups whole raisins
½ teaspoon salt
1 teaspoon mace
2 tablespoons each, cinnamon, cloves and allspice
2 whole nutmegs, grated
3 cups liquid in which meat was cooked
3 cups cider
½ cup vinegar
1 cup molasses
¾ pound citron, chopped
1½ cups chopped raisins
Juice of 2 lemons and 2 oranges
2 tablespoons lemon extract
1 teaspoon almond extract
1½ cups peach brandy

Cover meat with water and boil until tender, then chop. Mix all ingredients except brandy in order given in a large vessel. Simmer 1½ hours, then add brandy. Fill quart jars and seal according to canning directions. Let season at least one month before using. Use one quart for each pie, adding ¼ cup fruit brandy to the filling before baking the pie. This will bring out the flavor more. Place filling in a 9- or 10-inch pie pan, cover with a top crust and bake at 425 degrees for 40-45 minutes.

# Mountain Oysters

*Whether you call them calf fries or mountain oysters, there is no better treat after spring roundup.*

Calf testicles
Buttermilk
Flour
Oil for frying

Cut both outer skins off the calf testicles and cut into bite-size pieces. Dip in flour, then buttermilk, then again in flour. Deep fry in oil until golden brown and crisp. Serve with Louisiana Cocktail Sauce, Cajun Mustard Dip, or just plain ketchup

# Cajun Mustard Dip

*Lloyd Smith is a misplaced Louisianan now in Whittier, California. His mustard dip, which he uses for fried catfish, turns out to be a perfect complement for calf fries as well.*

2 cups mayonnaise
3 heaping tablespoons mustard
1 tablespoon garlic powder
2 teaspoons red pepper, or to taste

Mix all ingredients and let sit 1-2 hours before serving.

# Louisiana Cocktail Sauce

1 cup ketchup
$1/_3$-$1/_2$ cup horseradish
1 tablespoon Worcestershire sauce
Juice of $1/_2$ lemon
Tabasco sauce to taste

Mix all together and serve as a dip for Mountain Oysters.

# Sautéed Sweetbreads

*Mary Magoffin, Douglas, Arizona.*

1 pound sweetbreads
Vinegar and water
1 bay leaf
½ cup cornmeal
2-3 tablespoons vegetable shortening
Salt and pepper

To prepare sweetbreads, soak in cold water for at least 1 hour. Drain and cover with acidulated water (2 tablespoons vinegar to each quart of water). Add the bay leaf. Slowly bring to a boil and simmer 5-10 minutes. Drain and plunge the sweetbreads in cold water. When cool, trim by removing cartilage, tubes, connective tissue and tougher membrane. Cut into bite-size pieces and dredge in cornmeal. Heat shortening to hot but not smoking. Sauté the sweetbreads over moderate heat until golden brown on all sides. Sprinkle salt and pepper on as they cook.

# Phony Croghan Bologna

*Lillian Gorczyca, Humboldt, Arizona.*

2½ pounds ground beef
1 cup water
2 tablespoons liquid smoke
2 tablespoons quick salt
½ teaspoon onion powder
½ teaspoon garlic powder
¼ teaspoon mustard seed

Mix all ingredients well. Form into a long roll, wrap in foil with shiny side in, and refrigerate 24 hours. Bake on a rack for 1½ hours at 300 degrees. Cool and refrigerate.

# Uncle Tom's Homemade Beef Sausage

*Tom Cox, Sault Ste. Marie, Michigan.*

6 pounds ground beef.
6 teaspoons quick salt
4 teaspoons black pepper
2 teaspoons garlic salt
3 teaspoons mustard seed
3 teaspoons hickory smoked salt

Mix the meat and all spices together thoroughly as for a meat loaf. Cover and refrigerate for 24 hours. Mix again, cover and refrigerate another 24 hours. Mix again and shape into logs. Place on a broiler pan rack or cake racks, set in a jelly roll pan and bake at 250 degrees for 8 hours. Cool and keep refrigerated.

*This recipe is low in cholesterol and saturated fat if lean ground beef is used.*

# Aunt Bess's Liver

*Mary Magoffin, Douglas, Arizona, says her family thinks this is the* only *way to cook liver.*

1 pound calf or beef liver, cut in ½ inch slices, skin trimmed
½ cup cornmeal (in a pie plate)
Salt and pepper
2-3 tablespoons vegetable shortening

You will need two skillets, preferably iron, for this recipe. Put about 1 inch of water in one skillet and bring to a boil. Dip each slice of liver into the boiling water until it turns gray, then turn on the other side for the same length of time. Remove from the pan and coat both sides with cornmeal. Heat the shortening in the other skillet. Ease the coated liver slices into the hot shortening and sauté until the juices come through the cornmeal. Salt and pepper lightly. Turn with a spatula and cook about the same length of time on the other side. Serve immediately with ketchup or horseradish. Also good with sautéed onions.

# Liver with Sage Cream Gravy

4 slices calves liver, about 1 pound, ¼ inch thick
¼ cup flour
Salt and pepper
4 tablespoons unsalted butter
1 cup onions, chopped fine
2 cloves garlic, chopped fine
½ cup Marsala wine
3 tablespoons red wine vinegar
1-1½ cups cream
1 tablespoon sage, crushed
¼ teaspoon dried thyme
4 slices  prosciutto ham or bacon, fried crisp and crumbled

Salt and pepper the liver and coat lightly with flour. Heat
the butter in a heavy frying pan. Sauté the liver over medium high heat until barely pink inside, about 2-3 minutes
per side. Remove from pan and add the onion and garlic.
Cook, stirring occasionally until golden brown. Reduce heat
and deglaze the pan with the Marsala. Add the red wine
vinegar and cook about 1 minute. Add the cream, sage and
thyme, and adjust seasoning. Cook about 3 minutes. Serve
the sauce over the liver and top with crumbled prosciutto or
bacon. Serves 2-4.

# Mexican Liver

*Reprinted from the Lunt family cookbook,* What's Cookin' in Kathleen's Kitchen. *Author Olive Lunt of Pima, Arizona says, "Even liver haters will like this — if you don't tell them it's liver."*

1½ pounds thinly sliced liver
½ cup shortening or bacon drippings
4 onions, thinly sliced or chopped
4 tomatoes, peeled and sliced, or 1 28-ounce can tomatoes, sliced
1 teaspoon salt
¼ teaspoon pepper
¼ teaspoon curry powder
2 teaspoons or more chili powder
2 cups water

Fry liver until brown on both sides. Remove from pan and cut into thin strips. Put meat back into pan. Add all remaining ingredients. Cover and cook slowly about 30 minutes until sauce thickens slightly. Especially good served over rice. Serves 4-6.

# Grilled Liver Kabobs

1½ pounds calves' liver, cut in 1½-inch cubes
Salt and fresh ground black pepper
2 tablespoons fresh sage, chopped, or 2 teaspoons dried
1 tablespoon fresh rosemary, chopped, or 1 teaspoon dried
¼ cup red wine vinegar
¼ cup olive oil
12 slices bacon

Put liver in a shallow dish. Sprinkle with salt and pepper, sage and rosemary. Mix the oil and vinegar and pour over liver, stirring to coat. Marinate 1 hour, turning occasionally. Wrap each piece of liver with a half slice of bacon and thread on skewers. Grill over charcoal, brushing with the marinade, until browned but still pink inside.

ಬಂದ

# VEAL

ಬಂದ

# Veal with Asparagus

1 pound veal scallops
Salt and pepper to taste
3 teaspoon paprika
24 small, fresh asparagus spears, trimmed
4 tablespoons unsalted butter
2 tablespoons olive oil
1 cup coarse, fresh bread crumbs
4 tablespoons chopped parsley

Pound the veal thin and season with salt, pepper and paprika. Cook the asparagus in a large pot of unsalted boiling
water until tender, about 5 minutes. In a large skillet, melt 2
tablespoons butter and 1 tablespoon olive oil over medium
high heat. Sauté the scallops, turning once, until browned
and cooked through, 2-3 minutes per side. Remove the scallops and cover loosely with foil to keep warm. Add the remaining 2 tablespoons butter and 1 tablespoon oil to the skillet. When melted stir in the bread crumbs and cook, stirring
occasionally, until crisp, 5-10 minutes. Add parsley. Roll the
asparagus in the bread crumb mixture to coat, then divide
asparagus and veal between 4 places. Sprinkle remaining
bread crumbs, and pour any accumulated juices over the
veal. Serves 4.

*Veal scallops are low in saturated fat and cholesterol. This recipe is low
in saturated fat and cholesterol if unsaturated margarine is used instead
of butter.*

# Veal Marsala with Morels

*The morel, a type of mushroom grown in Europe, has a taste and texture quite different from the domestic mushroom. They are widely available, dried, in specialty food stores.*

¾ pound veal scallops
Salt and pepper
¾ ounce dried morels
2 tablespoons olive oil
3 tablespoons butter
1 tablespoon shallots, minced
⅓ cup Marsala wine
1 tablespoon beef broth concentrate
1 tablespoon cream

Pound the veal thin and season with salt and pepper. Soak the morels in warm water for 30 minutes and cut any large ones into bite size pieces. In a heavy skillet heat 2 table-spoons olive oil and 2 tablespoons butter. Add the veal and sauté over medium high heat until done, about 3-4 minutes per side. Remove from the skillet, add the shallots to the pan and cook until wilted. Reduce the heat and deglaze the pan with the Marsala. Allow to cook down slightly, then add the morels and ⅓ cup of their liquid. Stir in the beef broth concentrate, the cream and 1 tablespoon butter. Continue cooking until reduced to a medium thick sauce. Add the veal back to the pan to warm. Serve with the morels and sauce on top. Serves 2-4.

# Veal with Crawfish Creole Sauce

*This recipe is typical of the best of New Orleans style Creole cooking. If you can't get crawfish, use medium size shrimp.*

1 pound veal scallops
2 medium onions, chopped
2 bell peppers, chopped
2 ribs celery, chopped
2 cloves garlic, minced
8 tablespoons unsalted butter
1 28-ounce can tomatoes, chopped
¼ teaspoon cayenne pepper
4 tablespoons parsley, chopped
3 green onions, including tops, chopped
½-1 cup chicken broth
1 pound crawfish tails, or medium size shrimp
Flour for dusting veal
Salt and pepper to taste

Sauté the onions, peppers, celery and garlic in 4 tablespoons unsalted butter until wilted, about 5 minutes. Add the tomatoes, seasoning, parsley and green onions. Cover and cook about 10 minutes. Add chicken broth to thin sauce a little. Add the crawfish tails or shrimp and cook 15 minutes. Dust the veal scallops with flour and season with salt and pepper. Sauté in 4 tablespoons butter until browned and cooked through. Serve covered with the creole sauce. Serves 4.

# Raspberry Veal

4 boneless veal leg tip steaks (about 1 pound), pounded thin
Salt and pepper to taste
4 tablespoons butter
¼ cup finely chopped yellow onion
4 tablespoons raspberry vinegar
¼ cup chicken broth
¼ cup heavy cream

Melt 2 tablespoons butter in a heavy skillet. Add the veal steaks and cook over medium high heat about 3 minutes per side, or until lightly browned. Remove from the skillet and reserve. Add the rest of the butter and the onion. Cook covered over low heat about 5 minutes. Raise the heat and add the vinegar. Cook, stirring, until reduced to a spoonful of syrup. Stir in the chicken broth and cream and simmer about 1 minute. Return the veal to the pan and simmer in the sauce until it is done and the sauce has thickened slightly, about 5 minutes. Do not overcook. Serves 4.

# Veal Cilantro Over Fettuccine

1 pound veal scallops, cut in strips
1 medium onion, chopped
1 clove garlic, minced
3 tablespoons unsalted butter
3 tablespoons cooking oil
2 tablespoons flour
Salt and pepper to taste
Dash cayenne pepper
½ cup dry white wine
Juice of 1 lemon
¼ cup heavy cream
2 tablespoons fresh chopped cilantro

Heat the butter and oil in a large skillet. Sauté onion and garlic until wilted. Dust the veal strips with flour and add to the pan, cooking over medium high heat until lightly browned, about 5 minutes. Add salt, pepper and cayenne pepper to taste. Stir in wine and lemon juice, cooking and stirring until sauce thickens. Add cream and cilantro, and cook until heated through. Serve over fettuccine. Serves 4.

*This recipe is moderate in cholesterol and saturated fat if unsaturated oil or margarine is used instead of butter.*

# Veal Paprikash

*Judith Wood, Wood Brangus Ranch, Dallas, Texas.*

1 pound veal cutlets, sliced ¼ -inch thick
¼ cup very thinly sliced onions
3 tablespoons butter
¼ cup seasoned flour
1½ cups chicken stock
¾ cup sour cream
Paprika

Sauté onions in butter. Remove onions and brown cutlets that have been rolled in the seasoned flour. Add stock and onions, then simmer covered for 1 hour. Add sour cream, sprinkle with paprika and simmer until well blended. Serve over buttered fine noodles. Serves 4-6.

# Gettysburg Veal Casserole

*Olive Lunt, Pima, Arizona.*

4 pounds boneless veal, cut in 1-inch cubes
½ cup butter or margarine
½ teaspoon salt
⅛ teaspoon pepper
2 10-ounce cans cream of mushroom soup (undiluted)
3 cups sliced bacon
¼ teaspoon seasoned salt
⅛ teaspoon Tabasco sauce
1 cup sour cream
⅛ teaspoon cracked black pepper
Hot cooked rice

Heat ¼ cup butter in a large skillet. Add veal, half at a time, and brown well on all sides. Remove, as browned, to a large, deep roasting pan with a tight fitting cover. Sprinkle the veal with salt and ⅛ teaspoon pepper. Spoon mushroom soup over top. Preheat oven to 375 degrees. Heat remaining butter in same skillet. Add onion, sauté until golden brown and spread over meat in roasting pan. Add ¼ cup water, seasoned salt and Tabasco to skillet and bring to a boil, stirring to dissolve browned bits in pan. Pour over meat and onion. Bake, covered, 1 hour and 20 minutes. Remove cover. Add sour cream, sprinkle with cracked pepper, and stir gently just until blended. Bake uncovered, 10 minutes longer. Serve over rice. Serves 12.

# Veal Fricassee

2 pounds veal stew meat, cut in 1 inch cubes
6 tablespoons olive oil
1 large onion, chopped
4 garlic cloves, chopped fine
1 29-ounce can crushed tomatoes with puree
¼ cup fresh chopped basil leaves, or 1 tablespoon dried
½ cup fresh chopped parsley
1 tablespoon fresh chopped oregano, or 1 teaspoon dried
1 teaspoon salt
Fresh ground black pepper to taste
Dash of cayenne pepper, or to taste
1 cup heavy cream
Cooked noodles

Sauté the veal in 3 tablespoons olive oil until browned and set aside. To prepare sauce, sauté the onion and garlic in 3 tablespoons olive oil over moderate heat for 10 minutes. Add the tomatoes, basil, parsley, oregano, salt and pepper. Cook, covered, for about 20 minutes. Stir in the cream and cook until heated through. Transfer the veal to a baking dish and stir in the sauce. Bake, covered, for 2 hours, stirring occasionally. Serve over noodles. Serves 4-6.

# Veal Stuffed Beef with Orange Sauce

*This recipe took second place in the 1988 Arizona Beef Cook-Off for Dan Meinke, Tucson, Arizona.*

1½ pounds beef round steak, cut ½ inch thick
½ medium head cabbage, chopped
1 large green onion, chopped
3 large carrots, chopped fine
¾ pound ground veal
½ teaspoon thyme
½ teaspoon garlic powder
2 teaspoons seasoned salt
⅛ teaspoon cayenne pepper
1 tablespoon salad oil
1 cup beef broth
1 cup orange juice
1 tablespoon corn starch
1 tablespoon butter or margarine

Pound beef round steak until tender. Combine cabbage, onion, carrots and veal with thyme, garlic powder, seasoned salt and cayenne pepper. Mix together well. Spread mixture on one end of the round steak. Roll up and fasten with toothpicks. Heat oil in skillet, brown round steak roll on all sides. Place in the middle of a 13 x 9 inch pan. Pour beef broth over roll. Cover and bake in a 375-degree oven for 1½ hours. Remove beef roll from pan. Pour liquid into measuring cup to measure 1 cup. Discard remaining liquid. Pour 1 cup liquid in saucepan and heat slowly. In a bowl mix corn starch and orange juice, with pepper and garlic to taste. Bring liquid to a boil and slowly add orange juice mixture. Add 1 tablespoon butter and stir until thickened. Slice in 1-inch slices and serve with orange sauce. Serves 6.

# LEFTOVERS

# Refrigerator-Cleaning Day Egg Rolls

*This is how Karen Halford, executive secretary of the Barzona Breeders Association of America, Prescott, Arizona, uses up all the leftover beef and limp vegetables she finds in the back of her refrigerator on cleaning day.*

1½-2 cups pieces of leftover roast, stew meat or steak
2 stalks celery, chopped fine
3 carrots, peeled and grated
1 medium zucchini, grated
½ medium onion, chopped fine
¾ cup finely chopped Chinese cabbage core
1 tablespoon grated ginger (fresh or sugared, not powdered)
2 cloves garlic
Salt and pepper to taste
2 dozen egg roll wrappers
Peanut oil for frying

Put the meat in a food processor and grind into small chunks. Combine with all other chopped vegetables and a little water. Simmer 15 minutes, then let sit for 2 hours for flavors to mix. Roll about 1 tablespoon in each egg roll wrapper (or use wonton wrappers to make appetizers). Deep fry in peanut oil until golden brown, drain well and serve with apricot sauce. These can be warmed over in the oven.

*The use of lean beef makes this recipe low in cholesterol and saturated fats.*

# Apricot Sauce

½ cup apricot jelly
1 tablespoon margarine

Heat jelly and margarine in a small saucepan and serve over egg rolls.

# Beef Pâté

*Naomi Flowers, Baton Rouge, Louisiana*

1½-2 cups lean leftover beef
½ cup cooked ham or sausage, or ¼ cup bacon
¼ teaspoon onion powder
¼ teaspoon garlic powder
¼-½ cup soft bread crumbs
¼ cup snipped parsley
¼ teaspoon nutmeg
¼-½ cup thick barbecue sauce
2-4 tablespoons Worcestershire sauce
Shortening

Using a food processor, process the meat with the steel blade until the consistency of coarse crumbs. Add the rest of the ingredients and process to form a soft ball. Coat a small mold with shortening and pack the mixture into the mold. Refrigerate for at least 12 hours. Unmold and serve with assorted crackers. Serves 24.

# Tortilla Soup

*Use the leftover stock, sliced onions and chiles from Pot Roast Ranchera to make this delicious soup.*

2 quarts reserved stock with onions and chiles
1 cup cooked pinto beans, or 1 16-ounce can
1 16-ounce can corn, drained
1 cup tortilla chips, broken in bite-size pieces

Strain the grease off the soup stock. (The easiest way to do this is to refrigerate it until the grease rises to the top and hardens.) Add the other ingredients except for the tortilla chips, and heat through, adding more water if it seems too thick. Before serving stir in the tortilla chips.

# Second Day Roast Beef

*Sandy Smith, Douglas, Arizona*

1 pound cooked roast beef, sliced thin
2 cups brown gravy from roast drippings
4 tablespoons Burgundy wine
2 4-ounce cans mushroom stems and pieces
4 ounces cooked noodles
2 tablespoons parsley, chopped

Stir the roast beef, gravy, wine and mushrooms together and heat well. Serve over the noodles and sprinkle with parsley. Serves 4.

# Quick Stroganoff

*Marion Gary, Prescott, Arizona.*

3 cups cooked roast beef, cut into strips
2 tablespoons butter
½ cup chopped onions
½ cup beef stock or drippings from the roast
1 4-ounce can sliced button mushrooms
Salt and pepper to taste
1 cup sour cream
1 tablespoon flour

Trim excess fat from the roast and cut into strips. Heat butter in a heavy skillet, add onions and sauté until wilted. Add meat, salt, pepper and beef stock and cook slowly for 10 minutes. Add mushrooms. Just before serving dissolve flour in the sour cream and add to the beef mixture. Heat well until thick, but do not boil. Serve over rice or buttered noodles. Serves 6.

# Pot Pie Stew

*Karen Halford, Prescott, Arizona.*

4 cups leftover pot roast or stew, including gravy and
    vegetables
2 cups Longhorn cheese, grated
2 cups bread crumbs
2 9-inch pie crusts

Cut the meat and vegetables into medium size chunks and
divide between two pie crusts. Pour pan gravy over the top.
Mix the cheese and bread crumbs and sprinkle over the top
of each pie. Pies can be baked either with or without a top
crust. (The following recipe makes enough dough for one
pie with top crust and one without, or 3 crusts with no top).
Bake at 350 degrees for 25-30 minutes.

**Pie Crusts:**
2 cups flour
½ teaspoon salt
½ teaspoon baking powder
½ tablespoon sugar
¾ cup shortening
½ cup warm water
1 beaten egg
1 teaspoon vinegar

Sift dry ingredients together. Cut in shortening until the size
of small peas. Stir in water, egg and vinegar. Form into three
balls and roll out for two bottom crusts and one top.

# Dashboard Turnovers

*Also from Karen Halford, this is a great lunch idea for husbands on the run. Use the preceding Pot Pie Stew recipe to make turnovers instead of pies. Wrap in foil with shiny side to the inside. Place on the dashboard of your pickup on a sunny day and presto! Hot turnovers for lunch.*

# Deviled Roast Slices

*A real quickie from Judith Wood, Wood Brangus Ranch, Dallas, Texas, that is positively delicious. This recipe makes use of leftover roast beef, but it's so good, you could make a roast just for this alone.*

Cut ¼ -inch slices off the roast and spread both sides of each slice with your favorite mustard. Coat slices with bread crumbs and sprinkle with butter. Sauté in more butter until golden brown.

*This recipe is moderate in cholesterol and saturated fat if unsaturated margarine is used instead of butter.*

# Real Cowboys Will Eat This Quiche

*Anne Marie Moore, Rafter X Ranch, Elfrida, Arizona, invented this quiche that even "real cowboys" will eat.*

1 pound roasted brisket, shredded (or any other roast cut)
1 4-ounce jar diced pimentos
1 4-ounce can diced green chiles
1 4 ½ -ounce can sliced black olives
¼ pound Monterey Jack cheese, shredded
1½ cups milk
3 large eggs
¾ cup baking mix

Preheat oven to 400 degrees. Grease a 9- or 10-inch pie or quiche pan. Layer beef, drained pimentos, chiles, olives, and cheese in pan. Blend milk, eggs and baking mix 15 seconds in a blender and pour over other ingredients. Optional: sprinkle with paprika, ground pepper and/or parsley flakes. Bake for 30-35 minutes until an inserted knife comes out clean. Cut into 6 wedges for 6 servings, and serve with a crisp vegetable salad.

# On The Side

# Steak and Enchiladas

3 tablespoons oil
1 medium onion, chopped
1 clove garlic, minced
1 29-ounce can crushed tomatoes with puree
1 tablespoon fresh oregano, chopped, or 1 teaspoon dried
1-2 jalapeños, chopped fine
Salt to taste
12 corn tortillas
Oil for frying
1 pound Monterey Jack cheese, shredded
2 pints sour cream

To prepare sauce, sauté onion and garlic in 3 tablespoons oil until wilted. Add tomatoes, oregano, jalapeños and salt. Simmer over low heat for 20-30 minutes. Dip the tortillas in hot oil until just softened. Place a little sauce and cheese on each and roll. Arrange in a buttered shallow baking dish. Pour the remaining sauce over the enchiladas, top with the remaining cheese and spoon the sour cream over all. Bake at 325 degrees for 30 minutes. Serves 6-12 as a side dish with steaks.

# Steak and Spaghetti

¼ cup olive oil
1 cup onion, chopped
2-3 cloves garlic, chopped fine
1 28-ounce can crushed tomatoes with puree, or an equal
     amount of fresh tomatoes, peeled and chopped
1 8-ounce can tomato sauce
2 tablespoons fresh chopped oregano, or 2 teaspoons dried
1 tablespoons fresh chopped basil, or 1 teaspoon dried
1-2 dried hot peppers, crushed
1 pound spaghetti, cooked

Sauté the onion and garlic in the olive oil until wilted. Stir in
the rest of the ingredients and simmer 30 minutes to 1 hour.
Serve over spaghetti as a side dish for grilled or broiled
steaks.

# Steak and Cheese Grits

*Don't say you don't like grits until you have tried these. This
makes a wonderful side dish with steaks instead of the same old
baked potato.*

4 cups boiling water
1 cup quick grits
1 stick butter
¾ pound sharp cheddar cheese, shredded
Garlic salt to taste
2 beaten eggs
⅓ cup milk

Cook the grits in water 5 minutes. Stir butter and cheese into
grits. Add garlic salt to taste, the eggs and milk. Pour into
a greased casserole and bake 40 minutes to an hour at 375
degrees.

# Mexican Spoon Bread

*Ellyn Teskey of the Todd 2Y Ranch, Mayer, Arizona, says this is "muy sabrosa" with Mexican food. We think it's good with anything!*

1 16-ounce can creamed corn
1 4-ounce can chopped green chiles
1 cup cornmeal
2 eggs
¼ cup oil
2 cups shredded cheddar cheese

Mix all ingredients together and pour into a greased 9 x 9-inch baking dish. Bake at 350 degrees for approximately 35 minutes or until set. Serves 6-8.

# Potatoes with Caviar

*This is another unusual alternative to baked potatoes. Serve with roast beef or grilled steaks.*

4 medium red potatoes
½ cup heavy cream
Milk
Salt and pepper to taste
Oil for deep frying
½ pint sour cream
4 ounces red or black caviar

Bake the potatoes at 350 degrees until well done, 45 minutes to 1 hour. Remove and cut into halves. Scoop out the pulp with a small spoon, being careful to keep the shells intact. In a small bowl mash the pulp with the cream, salt and pepper, and enough milk to make a good consistency. Heat the oil to 400 degrees, drop the potato shells in and fry until golden brown and crisp. Drain well on paper towels. Meanwhile, keep the mashed potatoes warm, or reheat in the microwave. Fill the shells with the potatoes, top with a spoonful of sour cream, and add two or more teaspoons of caviar. Serves 6-8.

# Picante Sauce

5-6 large, ripe tomatoes
4 fresh green chiles, peeled, or 1 4-ounce can
1 small onion
3 or more fresh jalapeños
1 tablespoon fresh cilantro
1 teaspoon salt

Core tomatoes and drop in boiling water until the skins crack. Transfer to a bowl of cold water and slip off skins. Chop the chiles, onions, jalapeños, tomatoes and cilantro coarsely, or process individually in a food processor. (Do not over process.) Mix all ingredients together and refrigerate until ready to use. Serve with fajitas or grilled beef. Makes about 1 quart.

# Pico de Gallo

*Judith Wood, Wood Brangus Ranch, Dallas, Texas.*

2 ripe tomatoes, coarsely chopped
1 bunch green onions, finely chopped
2 avocados, diced
¼ cup chopped cilantro
Garlic salt, salt and pepper to taste
Juice of a large lime
Fresh jalapeño, minced, to taste (go easy!)

Mix together and chill. Serve with fajitas or any grilled meat.

# Circle J Fruit Compote

*Peggy Monzingo of the ZR Hereford Ranch, Benson, Arizona, was given this recipe by her Uncle Joe Richardson from the Pyramid Lake country of Nevada. Uncle Joe was a cowboy, and a wild horse and dude wrangler, and "to have seen him smoking the vilest looking and smelling cigars," she says, "you couldn't imagine he would take to this sort of food."*

1 quart fresh fruit in any combination, cut up
¼ cup frozen orange juice concentrate
¼ cup honey

In a large bowl, toss the fruit with the thawed orange juice and honey. Let stand in the refrigerator an hour or more to blend flavors. This will keep for quite awhile in the refrigerator without discoloring if you don't use bananas or apples. Canned fruit can also be used.

# Puerto Rican Rice

*Dr. Ray Rodriguez, Tucson, Arizona.*

1 10-ounce can beef bouillon
1 10-ounce can French onion soup
10 ounces (1 soup can full) of long grain ride
1 2-ounce package slivered or sliced almonds
6 tablespoons melted butter

Mix all together and bake, covered, for 1 hour at 350 degrees.

# Los Alamos Style Beans

2 pounds pinquito beans
3 teaspoons chili powder
2 teaspoons garlic powder
½ teaspoon ground cumin
2 medium onions, chopped
½ pound bacon, chopped
1 16-ounce can tomatoes
Salt and pepper to taste

Clean and wash beans. Cover with cold water and soak overnight. Combine all ingredients in a large pot and bring to a boil. Simmer until tender. Serves approximately 20.

# Horner Mountain Frijoles

2 pounds pinto beans
1 12-ounce package lean bacon, cut in ½ -inch squares
2 onions, chopped
3 large cloves garlic, chopped
4 teaspoons salt and more to taste
3 jalapeños, chopped
Red pepper to taste
1 small bunch fresh cilantro

Cover beans with water and bring to a rolling boil. Soak beans overnight or all morning, then return to boil, lower heat and simmer for one hour. Fry bacon in a separate pan, then add to the beans, along with some of the grease and all the other ingredients except cilantro and salt. Cook at least 2 hours more, adding salt after 1 hour and adding water as necessary. Add chopped cilantro just before serving. Serves 16-20.

# Lesley's Baked Beans

*Lesley Flowers, Baton Rouge, Louisiana*

1 gallon pork and beans
½ pound bacon
1½ cups mustard
4 ounces Worcestershire sauce
3 cups ketchup
½ pound brown sugar
½ pound onion, chopped
2 cups dark corn syrup
Chili powder to taste

Mix all ingredients except chili powder together and prepare oven at 250-300 degrees. Before putting mixture in oven, sprinkle chili powder over top lightly. Cook two hours. Excess will freeze very well for future barbecues. Serves 30.

# Guacamole

2 very ripe, medium avocados (preferably Haas)
Juice of ½ lime
2 tablespoons minced onion
1 jalapeño, minced (or to taste)
Salt to taste
1 tablespoon minced fresh cilantro

Mash the avocados with a fork, leaving the mixture lumpy. Stir in the remaining ingredients and serve immediately.

# ❧ Photo Index ❧

Page 147. Wayne Word, O RO Ranch.

Page 148. Left to right, James Reed, Logan Bates, Jamie Wood, KJ Kasun, Swayze McCraine, Beano Kimball, Bailey Kimball, Howard Mesa Ranch.

Page153. KJ Kasun, Campwood Cattle Company.

Page 155. Ed Ashurst, 10X Ranch.

Page 163. Dakota Falcon, O RO Ranch.

Page 168. Mike O'Haco, O'Haco Cattle Company.

Page 170. Texas cowboy, Babbitt Ranches.

Page 172. Clay Rodgers, Babbitt Ranches.

Page 177. Cisco Scott, O RO Ranch.

Page 182. Drew Timmons, O RO Ranch.

# ᔄ RECIPE INDEX ᔅ

www.ingramcontent.com/pod-product-compliance
Lightning Source LLC
LaVergne TN
LVHW051633080426
835511LV00016B/2323